Awareness | Discovery | Wholeness | Transformation

THE HAZELDEN RECOVERY HORIZON®

Just as life is no straight-edged path, so in recovery we are faced with a lifelong journey of hills to climb and valleys to descend. One constant is that we take a searching look at where we've been, where we are now, and where we're going. Our focus changes from awareness of a problem, to discovery of solutions, to the wholeness we can enjoy when solutions bring peace, to the kind of transformation that changes us at the deepest level of our beings.

Awareness, Discovery, Wholeness, and *Transformation.* The Recovery Horizon is Hazelden's commitment to supporting you no matter where you are in your own process of personal and spiritual growth.

DISCOVERY

Moving forward, always on the road to recovery, we discover more about the people we were before dysfunction or addiction became a part of our lives. New and confusing emotions fill our minds and hearts. But as we continue to work, we practice new living skills and explore ways to create different relationships, as a new self emerges.

I DESERVE RESPECT

Confronting and Challenging Shame

Lewis M. Andrews, editor

◣ HAZELDEN®

Hazelden Educational Materials
Center City, Minnesota 55012-0176

ISBN 0-89486-870-5

Editor's Note

   Hazelden Educational Materials offers a variety of information on chemical
dependency and regulated areas. Our publications do not necessarily represent
Hazelden's programs, nor do they officially speak for any Twelve Step organi-
zation.
   The Twelve Steps are reprinted with permission of Alcoholics Anonymous
World Services, Inc. Permission to reprint the Twelve Steps does not mean that
Alcoholics Anonymous has reviewed or approved the contents of this publication, nor that AA agrees with the views expressed herein. The views expressed
herein are solely those of the authors. AA is a program of recovery from alcoholism. Use of the Twelve Steps in connection with programs and activities
which are patterned after AA, but which address other problems, does not imply
otherwise.

Contents

Part I

Part II

PART I

Introduction: What Is Shame?

Lewis M. Andrews, Ph.D.

Lewis M. Andrews, Ph.D., is a research psychologist based in Redding, Connecticut, and is the author of the book To Thine Own Self Be True. *He is also the author of* Honesty and Happiness: Living from Your Personal Truth, *published by Hazelden. He writes and lectures widely on the topic of "Spiritual Values and Emotional Health."*

We all have moments when some unexpected event causes us to feel diminished and unworthy.

Imagine you are driving somewhere. You're going to work or perhaps you're on the way to pick up your child at school. It's a beautiful day; and so you've got the windows rolled down and you're playing a tape on the car's cassette machine. You find yourself singing along with your favorite song, when you pull up to a traffic light and come to a stop. Moments later you hear the sound of giggling. Looking over to the next lane, you realize that there are people sitting in the adjacent car and that they've been amusing themselves by listening to you hit all the wrong notes. Instinctively you turn red and dodge your head in embarrassment.

This is a relatively harmless case of feeling shame. Like the time we accidentally call our boss by the wrong name, get caught in a harmless exaggeration, or burp out loud in a movie theater, it's the kind of event we can later laugh about and, in the passing of days, we'll likely forget it ever happened.

Unfortunately, not all our experiences of feeling inadequate are as trivial. Some of us have childhood memories—getting caught while masturbating, or fumbling the catch that lost the big game—which leave us with an indelible feeling of worthlessness. Others of us have physical characteristics where we think we're too tall, too short, too thin, or too fat. Maybe we feel like we carry some social stigma, like being poor, uneducated, or out of work, that lead us to judge ourselves as being "useless," "trash," "a failure," or "unimportant" on a daily basis.

Many of us have such a devastating sense of shame about a past failure or humiliation or even membership in a socially disparaged religion, class, or ethnic group that we are simply unable to face it consciously. We repress our self-contempt, only to have it emerge in the form of crippling anxieties, addictions, and even physical ailments, such as allergies and headaches.

On one level, the field of psychology has always acknowledged people's feelings of shame. The world's first great psychologists—Freud in Europe and William James in America—lived in a time when people on both sides of the Atlantic were especially conscious of social etiquette and class distinction. During the nineteenth century, even the slightest departure from accepted manners and customs could cause an otherwise upstanding citizen to feel like a miserable failure.

But it has only been in the last few years that modern

psychology has come to appreciate the degree to which shame can devastate our emotional lives and the central role it appears to play in distorting our personal relationships. Recent research indicates that shame is a critical factor in the abuse of spouses and children, in depression, in narcissism, in phobias, in loneliness, in severe personality disorders, and even in the onset of suicidal thoughts.

Shame is especially present in the problems of alcoholism, drug abuse, gambling, compulsive overeating and other addictions. Not only are many people inclined to drink, take narcotics, or abuse other substances as a way to cope with their sense of shame, but the foolish and self-destructive acts they often commit while under the influence only add to feelings of humiliation. Addiction and shame have a chicken-and-egg relationship that continues to cycle out of control until some action is taken.

Fortunately, there is help. The Twelve Step program of Alcoholics Anonymous, which over the last decade has been an effective treatment for a wide variety of emotional problems, has proved especially useful in the taming of shame. Therapies compatible with the Twelve Step program, like Rational-Emotive Therapy, developed by Albert Ellis, offer added techniques that dramatically improve the quality of life, not only for recovering alcoholics and other addicts, but for all who suffer from the relentless contempt for themselves.

To make best use of the tools that are available, however, we must first have a clearer idea of what shame is and where it comes from. The essays in the first part of this book help us to distinguish shame from another

destructive emotion with which it is often confused—
guilt. Guilt is a negative feeling about the harm we've
caused to others; shame is a negative judgment about
our own basic worthiness. We'll also explore the different kinds of shame—about our needs, our bodies, our
feelings, our families—and where these withering self-
evaluations come from.

Armed with new insights we'll be ready to begin
breaking the habits of internal derision that deprive us
of the esteem and contentment which every human being rightly deserves. For the good news is that, no matter what circumstances may have originally led to our
destructive self-judgments, the power to change is
within our grasp. We not only deserve respect—we have
the capacity, in the end, to grant it to ourselves . . .
and to give it unconditionally.

Shame-Faced: Shame and Addiction

Stephanie E.

Stephanie E. is in a Twelve Step program, and has written several books and pamphlets on recovery. This is one of the classical pieces on shame and has helped many thousands of people recovering from addiction.

Shame and addiction are like Siamese twins. One rarely exists without the other. It would be hard to find an addict without shame—or a shameful person without some addiction. You could say that shame and addiction are attached at the heart, sharing the same blood that keeps them alive. Where one leads, the other must follow. Both exist behind walls of denial, growing like cancer, sucking out life. And both are destined to the same deadly spiral.

Shame's most important objective is *to not be exposed*. Most people who are "shame-based" don't know it. They can't. It's slippery. Sometimes it comes on so slowly, you won't know when you started to feel this way. And it is most often disguised as what it is *not*: irrational white rage, indifference, the overwhelming need to control, depression, confusion, flightiness, the obsession to use, numbness, panic, and the need to run. We will grasp whatever defense we can to survive slipping into the bottomless pit of shame.

Ironically, these very defenses saved us during our darkest moments. They may actually be the reasons we are alive today, and we can think of them as healthy reactions to very unhealthy circumstances. We can admire and respect ourselves for having them, before we lay them down and begin living a new life that no longer requires such reactions.

Most of us come into recovery as innocents. In the rawness of hitting bottom and accepting the First Step about powerlessness, we are like children, hoping everything will be fixed now. The reality is that getting sober merely gets us up to the starting gate. Eventually, if we are true to our recovery, we will collide with the feelings we ran from for years.

Recovery is not a destination. It is a journey. From the day we took our first sober steps, we began the lifelong journey toward serenity and, ultimately, love. The road is sometimes treacherous, sometimes glorious, and always unpredictable. It demands our entire participation, our full and total commitment from our core. But we cannot get there if we are shackled by shame. With shame running our lives, many of us will drink again, sadly concluding that "sobriety wasn't all it was cracked up to be." Many Al-Anons will stop going to meetings and slip right back into addiction because we can't imagine that anyone else has ever done the horrible things we've done when stone-cold sober.

Many of us will never return from a slip because the shame devours us, and death seems to be the only way to relieve the pain. Anyone who has experienced the depths of shame can understand how suicide may seem to be a kinder solution.

But there is another way. The first step is to recognize our shame. Exposure is the only way out. If you are reading this, you are already halfway home. The purpose of this is to give you new hope and a few tools to combat shame. Shame may be a universal emotion, felt by all human beings because we can never live up to the perfection and ideals of our limitless imaginations. But it serves no purpose other than to slowly kill us. This world would not be worse off without it.

Naked Exposure

Shame begins with feeling vulnerable and threatened. Out of control. Suddenly, we are exposed, and we are in danger of losing something, someone. When we are exposed against our will and our secrets are revealed, even before ourselves, we feel shame.

It can begin with a belief we formulated without even knowing it. Yet beliefs are not necessarily based on reality. They are, however, very real for us, personally. If we decided when we were very young that we were fools for loving a parent who left us, then it's possible to feel shame for the rest of our lives at the very thought of being left by someone. And so, we work very hard at not being found out. For most human beings, loving is as instinctual as sleeping and eating. But for the shamed person, loving means being out of control.

Frantically, we build elaborate defenses to make sure we are never found out. Never exposed. Imagine what that does to a relationship. There can be no intimacy when we will not reveal ourselves, not declare ourselves, not commit ourselves. That is the result of shame. Eventually, our partner will leave, frustrated and confused. And we will have what we so desperately tried to protect ourselves from: rejection.

Intimacy requires that we be vulnerable, out of control. The alcoholic personality has an aversion to being out of control. After all, didn't we drink to gain control over our feelings? Yet we cannot accept love without giving up control. In order to accept love we must sit still. We must be quiet. And we must open our hearts to someone else, who accepts us, in all our humanness.

It sounds wonderful. But for the shame-based person, it feels horrendous. Being loved means being exposed. And being exposed means being out of control.

The Cave-In

Shame separates us from others, from God, and from ourselves. It strangles our belief in a Higher Power. And without spirituality, we are profoundly alone in the world. How many times during our drinking careers did we really believe God had forgotten us? Even into sobriety, it is easy to slip back into controlling behavior for fear that God either isn't paying attention to us, or doesn't know what He/She is doing. And if we are truly honest, we'll admit we don't always trust God.

To be ultimately, universally alone is so devastating that most human beings run from it. It is a phenomenon all people face at one time or another in their lives. It is part of the human condition. Facing ourselves, our own emptiness, our own humanness, is terrifying. Yet for those of us who have battled with shame, we fear we will never survive the confrontation.

The Paralysis

Shame demands that we *do* something, immediately, because survival is at stake for the shamed person. So it is understandable that we respond with a knee-jerk reaction. And so we become desperate slaves to our feelings of shame; jumping when we're commanded to jump, and losing all sense of self in the meantime.

These are the feelings of shame. They depict the process that strips us of everything we know about ourselves and the world. We may feel it only once in a while, or we may live in a constant prison of shame. The fact is that shame robs us of our personal growth, of spiritual consolation, and of relationships which die for lack of intimacy. We long for intimacy, yet have no way of accepting it. Like starving children who cannot keep food down, shame strips us of all the nutrients we need to be whole human beings. Shame keeps us from loving and from being loved by others. It makes spontaneity impossible because we are so self-conscious. And it seems to be the first step to giving up on life. We who know shame know it is possible to die from it. Why else would we run so hard and fast from it? Why else would we be so terrified? Why else would we abuse ourselves and others to avoid it?

Shame is simply the other side of intimacy, of acceptance, and ultimately, of spirituality.

Out of Control

Somewhere, sometime, all of us in recovery had admitted to one fundamental shortcoming: that we were powerless over alcohol and that life for us was, indeed, unmanageable. In the First Step, Alcoholics Anonymous encourages us to remember the desperate groping for control of our drinking; how many times we promised ourselves: "Only one tonight," or "I don't think I'll drink/snort/shoot/smoke today." Then before we knew it, we were waking up in remorse, wondering why in God's name we couldn't use like normal people.

It took years for us to admit that our inability to control our chemical use was a serious problem. We fell short of the mark over and over, until we'd worn a path to hell. Our families tired of hearing the words, "I'll never do it again. . . ." But no matter how we tried, we could not keep our promises. We could not drink like normal people. Secretly, we thought we were deeply defective.

What few of us learn until we are very old and wise is that all human beings are born with shortcomings—everyone. And most people without addictions, who grow up in healthy families, learn to deal with this—even learn to laugh at themselves. Their sense of well-being comes from accepting themselves for *not* being perfect and from being accepted by their family for not being perfect. But in the chemically dependent family, we could not afford to be imperfect. Very often, our minor mistakes were treated like felonies, and the punishment was often very shaming and abusive. And so, for most of our lives, and even into sobriety, we try and try to be perfect human beings, living perfect lives, doing everything perfectly.

It's our innocent, childlike belief in perfection that sets us up to fall into shame. As members of the human race we will always fall short of perfection. If someone had told us, when we were young and still forming our belief systems, that no one is perfect and that's okay, we probably wouldn't expect so much of ourselves. But since many of us learned to be loved by how perfect we could be, *not* being perfect meant *not* being loved. Or not being successful. Or not being a whole human being.

The Twelve Steps of AA teach us that to be human is to be limited. Not less. Not unlovable. Not bad. Just human. We can never be perfect, or free of all character defects. We will always be working on them, for we strive for progress rather than perfection. When we strive for perfection, it is our shame trying to fortify us from ever having to be vulnerable.

Yet, acknowledging our shortcomings actually makes us more approachable—even more lovable. In AA, we thrive on our differences as well as our similarities. This is how we nurture individuality. We work our own programs, and learn from people we never dreamed we'd listen to under other circumstances because they are so different from us. Yet they may have something of great importance to give us in that meeting. AA provides a safe environment where differences are tolerated, and where we learn to take responsibility, not someone else's inventory.

There is a temptation in being different. We all want to be unique. To call an alcoholic "moderate" can actually hurt his or her ego. Some of us actually think that being called "eccentric" is a compliment. But being different is a double-edged sword; "being unique" sets up walls that closed us in during our using days. We believed no one knew what we were going through, so we could talk to no one, ask no one for help. In sobriety we need to guard against these feelings that might keep us from sharing with our sponsor, or going to a meeting. Feeling unique can be one of the red flags going up when we're on a dry drunk or ready for a wet one.

Somewhere there is a balance between holding on to our individuality and knowing we are all alike inside, sharing the same feelings and problems in life. That is the beauty of AA. We learn others feel the same things we feel. This is how we come to accept that we are really not alone. Accepting a Power greater than ourselves in the Second Step brings us new strength. *"Came to believe that a Power greater than ourselves could restore us to sanity."*

The word *sanity* has its root in the Greek word meaning "to be whole"; therefore the Second Step can be interpreted as the beginning of becoming whole again. It brings us acceptance, tolerance, and a Higher Power. In a moment of joy I can look at my inventory and exclaim, "I am perfectly imperfect!" I can love myself for it. When I am depressed, however, I can look at the same inventory and find evidence to prove, beyond a shadow of a doubt, that I am not a worthwhile human being. Not one of us *likes* being imperfect, but this is the universal human condition.

The Second Step teaches us that our Higher Power plays an active part in our lives as chemically dependent people, if only we will allow it. After time in sobriety we learn the effortless feeling of surrendering control over the outcome of events. We hear over and over, "You are responsible for the effort, not the outcome."

But at first, we have no idea what that means. Belly up? Give up? Let other people do it for you? No. None of these things. It comes from a growing sense of faith in our Higher Power's abilities to work miracles in our lives. Eventually, the second half of the Eleventh Step starts to make sense to us: "*praying only for knowledge of His will for us and the power to carry that out.*"

This is where we come to understand the real meaning of serenity: *Not the absence of problems, but the presence of God.* We learn that the serenity of sobriety doesn't mean we will someday be without problems. Serenity means we'll be able to face life's problems with a sense of well-being we've never had before. This comes effortlessly sometimes, and with great effort other times. Why?

Perhaps it has to do with "control" versus "responsibility." To be controlling doesn't necessarily mean we are being responsible. We can rationalize that we're taking care of business, and if we don't do it, no one will. But this isn't being responsible in the truest sense of the word. To control means we'll go to any lengths to have things the way we want them. In doing so we have no faith in a Higher Power's presence in our lives. It is a lonely and desperate place. To be responsible, however, means we will do the work that needs to be done, without focusing our eyes on the outcome. It means accepting that what we want and what we need may not always be the same. It means showing up. It means consistency. It means accountability. And it means accepting the outcome as what is really best for us.

Controlling is a defense of shame. It is important to realize our defenses didn't go away when we laid down our drugs. On the contrary, defenses will often rear their ugly heads stronger than ever in recovery. It's part of the healing process.

Sometimes our character defects get worse right before they start getting better. So, we'll smoke more, eat more, shut down more, rage more. We will do anything in excess in order *not* to look at what is right on our heels. It's the chemically dependent person's first nature to run when there's trouble. It's our new second nature to turn around, square-shouldered, and face those damned devils that have haunted us all of our lives. Like any skill, it must be practiced before it comes naturally. For some it may come easily. For others it may take awhile. But then, God only gives us as much as we can handle. . . .

AA teaches us that being human means that even with our limitations, we can continue to dream of a better life. Hope is looking at tomorrow and knowing it will be even better than today. It is knowing God has wonderful things in mind for us, if only we will let Her/Him have the steering wheel. And somehow, along the road of AA, we learn that the only way to serenity is through acceptance of ourselves, as we are, now.

Opening Up

To ask us about our shame while we're experiencing it is like trying to discuss the nature of convulsions with an epileptic during a seizure. The very nature of shame is to protect itself from exposure. So opening up during a severe attack of shame may seem impossible for some of us. Thus we become slaves to shame, staying loyal to the feelings, and ultimately, just trying to survive. The end result is that we withdraw into ourselves and become untouchable, unreachable.

Ironically, defenses probably saved our lives in our earlier years. Many of us grew up in abusive homes with shaming parents, and our only means of survival was to isolate, through fighting, freezing, or fleeing. So we can look at shame as actually serving us at one time in our lives.

On the other side of that coin, however, shame also kept us from trusting anyone. Without trust we had no way of being loved. And without love, we had no food for our souls. So we spent most of our lives unnurtured. Many of us have feared we were incapable of letting others love us. To sit still and actually accept loving can make us feel terribly vulnerable. Sometimes tenderness feels more like a searing, hot bath than what the fairy tales promised. We can take only so much, and then it's time to withdraw again into ourselves where it is safe; where we have control over our world.

Because we're isolated we don't know we're not unique, weird, crazy, or bad. We don't allow others in. Instead, we can end up living in a world that borders on paranoia, thinking if anyone ever knew our real feelings they would also know how defective we are. We start accepting our brutal self-criticism as normal. We become so accustomed to pain and self-abuse that the next logical step is to use alcohol and other drugs to ease the pain, the fears, and the loneliness of shame.

The Shame Spiral

Shame often sneaks up on us when we least suspect it, and we think we'll never feel good again. In truth, however, the stage gets set. To be vulnerable to a "shame attack," we must already be hiding some feelings from ourselves. Understanding what happens before, during, and after an attack of shame is an important step in gaining freedom from it. Because shame is so illusive, so evasive, it is imperative we know the clues, particularly when we are first beginning to identify shame. After a while, we will be able to catch ourselves when we fall into shame, and deal with it before it takes another piece of our soul. But understanding is just the first step. It cannot take the place of action, which we will talk about later.

There are many theories about shame. From Freud to Sartre, from Nietzsche to Shakespeare, much has been said about shame. It is a mysterious and controversial feeling, which some argue is the essence of the human condition, and others believe is totally useless. Nonetheless, there is a method to the madness of shame. It follows a certain pattern, not unlike the downward spiral of addiction. Here is one description of the shame spiral.

1. The bond between us is broken.
2. I am exposed—I fear abandonment.
3. I widen the chasm because I go away to hide.
4. I abuse—myself, or others.
5. The one who shamed me, or who I think shamed me, tries to approach me.
6. I feel even more exposed.
7. I throw up my defense: fight, freeze, or flee. I get rageful, numb, controlling, perfectionistic, etc.
8. The shamer retreats in self-preservation and the chasm widens.
9. I feel abandoned. I was right. I am no good.
10. More shame, more isolation, more abandonment, ad nauseam.

What are the things we feel shameful about? Most often, they are so deeply buried it's hard to unearth them. "I am unlovable because my mother told me to go away," "Daddy left because I was a bad girl," "I'm inadequate because I couldn't get Daddy to stop drinking," are common feelings of shame from our past. Whatever "tape" you have, it still has the same effect. One small thing, an innocent joke from a colleague, a statement of fact from a friend, can hook right into that tape of ours and zap! We've fallen into the shame mire. Sometimes we don't even need an outside stimulus, we can hook into it with our own negative messages.

Getting an idea of what your tape is will give you protection later on. Eventually, you won't display your buttons so others can come along and push PLAY. And though we are only allowed limited control in this life, this is one area in which we can begin to take some control.

Shame and Abandonment

Many of us have known shame since the cradle. Often we were "bad"; disciplined by having loving responses withheld as punishment. Some of us heard ridiculous things like, "No, I am not going to hold you because you're a bad girl." And so, being bad meant being abandoned. And in a child's small world, abandonment means death.

Shame and abandonment are closely related. Shame attaches itself to many situations and is different for each person. But almost always, when we peel away the layers of fear, abandonment is at the foundation of our shame.

If we are children of alcoholic or other shame-based families, we were abandoned. Rarely are alcoholic or codependent parents emotionally and spiritually present for their children. Most often they are too wrapped up in their own problems, trying to survive, and are unable to be available for their children. Abandonment may be as subtle as not being mentally present, or as obvious as a parent physically leaving the child. But in the end, the results are the same. The fear of abandonment becomes indelibly imprinted on our personalities, often controlling us for the rest of our lives.

Over many years shame itself becomes an addiction born out of loss of control. It is compulsive and all-consuming like alcoholism. It creates such self-consciousness that all spontaneity is lost. It has a spiral, like chemical addiction. The more shame we feel, the easier it is to abuse ourselves or others and feel more shame.

Recovering from addiction is also recovery from shame because it brings with it a sense of well-being that we have never known. In *Alcoholics Anonymous* the promises of recovery are listed.*

- We are going to know a new freedom and a new happiness.
- We will not regret the past nor wish to shut the door on it.
- We will comprehend the word serenity and we will know peace.
- No matter how far down the scale we have gone, we will see how our experience can benefit others.
- That feeling of uselessness and self-pity will disappear.
- We will lose interest in selfish things and gain interest in our fellows.
- Self-seeking will slip away.
- Our whole attitude and outlook upon life will change.
- Fear of people and of economic insecurity will leave us.
- We will intuitively know how to handle situations which used to baffle us.

*Alcoholics Anonymous World Services, Inc., *Alcoholics Anonymous*. (New York: Alcoholics Anonymous World Services, Inc., 1976) 83-84. Reprinted with permission of AA World Services, Inc.

• We will suddenly realize that God is doing for us what we could not do for ourselves.

It takes a belief in a Power greater than ourselves to enter recovery from addiction, so that we find the promises of AA coming true in our lives. One look at the Twelve Steps of AA reveals that seven of the Steps talk of work with our Higher Power. And as we walk the road of recovery from our addictions, we are simultaneously healing from the wounds of shame. The Twelve Step program is a simple solution for a very complex set of problems.

Doing Versus Being: The Difference Between Guilt and Shame

As we mature in recovery we learn to define our varying emotions. In early recovery it's not unusual for emotions to be all mixed up; therefore we are unable to understand the subtle shadings between feelings. But it is important to recognize these differences so we can begin to take care of ourselves. We will never be without feelings, and we can't necessarily control them. But we learn in recovery that when we take responsibility we have more choices. Sometimes, choices we never dreamed we'd have.

Shame and guilt are two very different emotions. Guilt is the simplest to understand and recognize. It's an action emotion. It's the beginning of amends. It stems from doing something we know is wrong; like stealing, lying, or cheating. Guilt happens to us when we break clear, specific rules. And the degree of guilt we feel is equal to the crime. If I cheat at cards I will feel twinges of guilt. If I cheat on my spouse I will probably feel more than a twinge. To make things confusing, guilt and shame often exist over the same incident. If I cheat at cards I may feel guilt about the cheating, and shame that I am such a rat I would do anything to win. But these feelings can be independent of each other too.

Shame is, as we've mentioned before, a more insidious chameleon, taking the form of everything it is not—rage, shutting down, controlling, depression, rigidness, numbness, etc. Sometimes we call embarrassment "shame." But people rarely commit suicide because they were embarrassed. No one likes being exposed, and that is about all that shame and embarrassment share.

Shame doesn't require that we *do* anything wrong. Shame is about our *being*. It isn't prompted by what we do, but rather by what we *are not*. "I'm no good at this game." "I'm so stupid." "I'm sorry I was so needy last night." Often, we're shamed by involuntary things. Someone doesn't love us to the same degree we love them. We showed up at a party inappropriately dressed. We could not keep a marriage together for our children. The core of shame is the lack of control we have. Shame surrounds that area of human existence where all human beings lack control, where human willpower is simply not enough. And where we fall short of the mark. Often, ironically, the more trivial the failure the deeper the shame.

The most simple way to distinguish between our guilt and our shame is to think of *guilt* as the feeling we get when we've broken a rule. Any rule. We know we shouldn't have done something. Then think of *shame* as not measuring up. Not meeting someone else's expectations of us. That someone could be as big as all of society or the man on the street. Shame charges us with being inadequate as a person. Shame comes when we feel we've fallen short of some imaginary mark set up to measure our worthiness as a person. It's usually a reaction far greater than the crime. And when we're consumed with shame we either fight, freeze, or flee, because our survival is at stake in our subconscious. That means we shut down, get overly busy, become rageful, go numb, become arrogant, or lie in a fetal position. Whatever defense we've constructed to survive, it keeps us unreachable and isolated.

It is important to respect our defenses, and not try to shame ourselves for having them. We do not need to complicate matters more. We will come out at the pace we need to. We know in our heart of hearts when we are willing to risk dropping a defense. And we must do it at our own pace. It only takes willingness. Our Higher Power will do the rest at the pace we can handle.

Being the imperfect perfectionists that we are as alcoholics, it isn't unusual to fall short of our own goals and expectations. This can continually reinforce our shame and keep us from gaining acceptance of our human sides, our flaws, and our strengths. And without acceptance, we cannot have serenity.

It's been said that guilt is: *I didn't do enough*. And shame is: *I am not enough*. Accepting that we can't do a thing about "not being enough" for someone else, is the beginning of recovery. We can accept ourselves as enough for us. This we have control of. In AA we learn that it is more than just "okay" to have shortcomings. We learn that grace is accepting ourselves as we are.

Regaining Dignity

> God, grant me the serenity
> To accept the things I cannot change,
> Courage to change the things I can,
> And wisdom to know the difference.
> —SERENITY PRAYER

The defenses we've learned while running from our shame have been self-preserving, desperate attempts to regain our dignity. Unfortunately, many of those behaviors have not worked to regain that dignity. Instead, we're frequently caught in self-abusive patterns with food, sex, or emotional binges. Like any other addiction, we promise ourselves we won't do it again. Then we do it again. Then we feel remorse. Then we punish ourselves more by continuing to do that which we're ashamed of doing. Regaining our dignity is a long process; not one that happens overnight, but one that will be our saving grace from the agony of shame.

The road to recovery from shame lies in the first five Steps of AA.

Admitting powerlessness over our shame. This is very different from helplessness. When I am helpless, I have no choices. When I am helpless, I have no power and I have no hope. But when I admit powerlessness, I gain the freedom of choice back. Paradoxically, I begin to regain my power in the act of surrendering.

Believing that a Power greater than ourselves can

restore us to sanity. Shame is very narcissistic. When we are in our shame, we are often grandiose enough to believe we are beyond hope. We are so focused on ourselves that we wouldn't be able to see a Higher Power if it reached out and shook our hand. Turning our eyes outward, to a source that we trust, a Power greater than ourselves, be it our AA group, an Al-Anon group, a sponsor, or a therapist, is a beginning of regaining hope. Later, it is the hope we gain from this leap of faith that will accompany us into the darkness ahead when we face our shame head-on.

Turning our will and our lives over to a Power greater than ourselves. Because shame is as slippery, as cunning, baffling, and powerful as our addiction, it is very important to not try and go it alone. In fact, if it were possible to recover from shame without help, we would have done it long ago. But since the nature of shame is to isolate us, we are hardly equipped to deal with it alone. Recovering from shame requires that we risk exposure. And we have every right to carefully choose the people we will expose ourselves to.

Making a fearless moral inventory. This is a very tricky Step for us: we can use it to beat ourselves up or we can use it to heal. It is important to do this Step after we've gained a spiritual base. In a fearless moral inventory, we look at our strengths as well as our character defects. It is important to look at each one of these with a goal in mind: to heal. If we think of these defects as the chains that keep us from spiritual freedom, rather than permanent limitations, we can more easily face our monsters. The importance of this Step comes in the exposure of our demons, for they are seldom as bad in the light of day as they are in the dark recesses of our minds. It is essential that we remove the shame from inside us, and put it outside where we can deal with it.

Admitting to God, to ourselves, and to another person the exact nature of our wrongs. The last step made us take the shame from inside and put it on the outside; in other words, expose it to ourselves. In this Step, we actually expose it to God and another person, so that we can be free of it. Admitting it to ourselves is not enough. We are too vulnerable to the power of shame. So finding someone who is trained in receiving Fifth Steps is essential. It is okay to interview this person first, to see if you feel you can trust him or her. Be overly protective of yourself, the way you would be if you were in charge of the welfare of a battered child. You are that battered child. And you deserve a non-shaming Fifth Step experience.

These five Steps are the beginning of a very important move away from the self-degradation that keeps us from serenity in sobriety. Looking to God, to our sponsors, or to a therapist, are some of the ways we can begin to become whole again.

Each day we can apply the principles of AA and Al-Anon to our shame. "Just for today, I will. . . ." And each day we can attempt to do just one thing differently. For each time we do something differently, we are one step farther away from the shame that threatens our sobriety, serenity, and spiritual growth.

Rule: Be Gentle with Yourself

Many of us have been brutal with ourselves. Perfectionism is yet another one of the hooks that can snag us back into shame. Gentleness with ourselves is one of the first steps in healing. This may mean giving ourselves a wide berth when it comes to making mistakes. We may repeat the same behavior over and over again, even though we don't intend to. It's important to remember that even when we seem to regress, it is only our unique way of going forward. Think of each act, both positive and negative, as a way our Higher Power has arranged for us to heal. As we start to develop self-forgiveness, we may have to do it over and over until we get it right. I had to think of myself as the four-year-old who had been emotionally wounded. I literally thought of her as my own child, imagining how I would treat her if she were in such pain. I imagined how I would support her when she was taking some very scary risks. I even imagined myself holding her when she was hurt or scared.

To this day she is real to me. Perhaps she will always be real. But the important thing is that she was the way I could begin to be gentle with myself. She was the beginning of self-forgiveness. When I didn't do things perfectly, when I failed at my attempts to pull out of shame, I began to forgive myself and try again. This was a major shift in behavior for me. Making mistakes had meant failure and rejection. In my family, if you made a mistake, you were shamed and there was no way out. I can't tell you what a relief it is now to be able to make mistakes and accept myself anyway. Today

I am much more productive, and I have fewer problems taking risks.

Al-Anon

When I hurt badly enough, I was finally able to accept the gift of Al-Anon. Many people in Al-Anon are intimately acquainted with shame. And Al-Anon offers one more way to heal by the mutual sharing of problems related to shame. As in our recovery from chemicals, we must not isolate ourselves. We need to be told the things we forget when we need them most, like *Easy Does It, One Day at a Time, First Things First,* and *This Too Shall Pass.* We need to know that others have been in the same pain, have done the same things, and are living full and whole lives in recovery. Al-Anon is a lovely, safe place to begin the healing process.

Therapy

It's important to consider therapy for shame; a therapist trained in recovery from shame can be very helpful. My therapist played a vital role in my recovery. I needed someone with whom I could build a relationship, risk exposure, and ask for reassurance in a healthy way. It was a chance to be parented the right way, and to learn to trust someone completely. And it was important that she kept the big picture in mind for me because I lost track of anything outside of my own immediate surroundings. Therapy may not be the only way, but it worked for me.

Ways to Combat Shame

There are concrete things to do to get out of shame and regain hope. We can choose to listen to new messages. Just reading this book is a way of finding new and different messages.

The next few suggestions are immediate ways of dealing with shame. They do not represent an alternative to therapy. Recovery is a complicated and sometimes long process, and it doesn't matter where you start—it's just important to start somewhere.

Getting a Shame Sponsor

If you are in a Twelve Step program, you know about sponsorship. Chances are, too, that if you are shame-based, you probably don't have a sponsor, or you probably don't use the one you have. When it comes to choosing a shame sponsor, you can apply the same rules you have followed in AA.

First, choose someone who has worked on shame and is further along than you are—someone who has something you want. This person doesn't have to be like you, but should be someone you feel comfortable moving through your discomfort with. Pay attention to your inner feelings about trustworthiness. If you don't trust someone for some reason, don't try to talk yourself out of this gut reaction. Instead, look for someone with whom you don't have to struggle.

It is also recommended that we choose a sponsor of the same sex. We might get distracted by issues that are bound to arise when we're dealing with the opposite sex, particularly when it comes to shame.

The next step is to use your sponsor. Many of us have gone as far as asking someone to be our sponsor, and then we never showed our faces at that meeting again. Remember, recovery from shame means risking exposure. We begin to heal when we see that people will not cringe and turn away when they see the real us. Instead, as we let people in, we will begin to learn how lovable we really are. A simple nod from others that lets us know they've been there, too, can be the beginning of freedom from our shame.

Doing a First Step on Shame

When we first got sober, admitting our powerlessness and acknowledging the ways our lives had become unmanageable were very important steps to our recovery. Painful as it was, our decision to turn our will and lives over to a Higher Power was reinforced by our acceptance of the First Step. We allowed a spiritual experience to happen to us. We surrendered in order to win.

The same is true of our shame. Looking at the various ways we have allowed shame to control us will give us the opportunity to be active players in our lives. Learning about our unmanageability sharpens our intuition and wisdom.

Affirmations

For most of our lives negative, self-defeating messages were the only ones we heard. We learned to carry forth the messages we heard as children into adulthood. Beating up on ourselves has become a habit we need to break. And so, affirming we're okay on a daily basis is more than just a luxury. It's vital.

If you are at all attached to your shame you will probably be embarrassed, at first, by these affirmations. But a sense of humor helps, and do remember to be gentle with yourself as you're learning.

These affirmations are very helpful in changing the messages you give to yourself. They are guides; not the gospel. You can make up your own as you go along.

I am a child of God and I deserve love, peace, prosperity, and serenity.

I am loved because I deserve love.

I forgive myself for hurting myself and others.

I forgive myself for letting others hurt me.

I forgive myself for accepting sex when I wanted love.

I am willing to accept love.

I am not alone. I am one with God and the universe.

I am whole and good.

I am innocent and totally deserving of love unconditionally.

I am capable of changing.

Just for today, I will respect my own and others' boundaries.

Just for today, I will be vulnerable with someone I trust.

Just for today, I will take one compliment and hold
it in my heart for more than just a fleeting
moment. I will let it nurture me.
Just for today, I will act in a way that I would admire
in someone else.

Repeating these affirmations can be a strong rein-
forcement of our inner selves. Writing them daily, in a
journal, is helpful. And, down the road, we can look
back and see how far we've come.

Spirituality

> It is the wounded oyster that
> mends itself with pearl. . . .
> RALPH WALDO EMERSON

Recovering from shame means that we have to regain
confidence in our Higher Power. It means that we come
to believe in our hearts that we are deserving children
of that Higher Power, who only wants the best for us.
Most of us have felt abandoned, even by God, and re-
pairing that relationship can make all the difference in
our recovery. Taking the Third Step on shame, believing that God would like to relieve us of that debilitating
emotion, and then turning it over to God, is one important way we can free ourselves.

Imagine a happy life, a life of serenity and love. It's
important for us to believe we can have this in order
for it to become a reality. And somehow, somewhere,
it will begin to make sense to us. Perhaps no one suffers
without a reason—not a punishing reason, but a healing

reason. Even those who are incapable of being honest with themselves teach us very important lessons. No alcoholic has ever died in vain. Because, somewhere, one of us woke up and recovered as a result.

We can take comfort in knowing our pain is not an exercise in self-mutilation, but rather part of the healing process. Not a day goes by that I can't look back, and know I am a better person for having had hardships. I wish them on no one, and I wouldn't want to face them again. But I am stronger now, having survived and recovered, for I know today I have more choices than I ever dreamed of. And hopefully, someday, I can help someone else who needs a little hope.

Putting Will In Its Place

Sometimes life seems so easy, like riding a bike downhill. And other times it seems like we're stuck in a swamp. When our will and God's are in concert, life is wonderful. Understanding which "will" to turn over is one of the mysteries every alcoholic would like to unravel. And perhaps it is as simple as "my will" versus "God's will." Only when we are ready do we get the benefit of God's will for us.

The belief that alcoholics have no willpower is a laughable myth. It took great will to hide our addictions, to continue working through years of morning hangovers. How else would we have been able to survive the horrendous situations of our drinking days? It is not will we are lacking; it is the ability to know the difference between our will and God's will. It is through the Twelve Steps of AA, the warmth and safety of our meetings, and the Serenity Prayer that we learn what we *can* control. And then, one day, suddenly, it all makes sense: we realize the promises of AA have come true. For recovery from shame is recovery from our addictions; it is freedom from the prison walls that keep us from living our lives to the fullest, and loving our loved ones to the limits of our hearts.

There is hope. We should never give up on hope.

Body Image:
From Shame to Love

Guy Kettelhack

Guy Kettelhack is also the author of How to Make Love While Conscious, *the Sobriety 1, 2, 3 series, coauthor of* Step Zero, *and many other titles. He lives in New York, New York.*

When we come into recovery, at least via the Twelve Step route, we often hear that addiction is a physical, mental, and spiritual disease. If you're like me and many of the people I've listened to, you probably quickly glossed over the "physical" part. "Yeah," you might have dismissed all that to yourself, "I sure was a mess." Sleeplessness, chronic diarrhea, kidney or liver disease, obesity, high blood pressure, heart problems: it's no secret how physically ravaging addiction can be. My revelation, as I've gone on in recovery, is that addiction is a physical disease in ways that go beyond our outward state of bodily disrepair. Something even more basic is at stake. Something that has to do with accepting that we *exist* as physical bodies. Most of us—whether before, during, or after our active drinking and drugging lives—had and have some formidable problems facing our physical selves. Most of us have learned to feel a terribly damaging reflexive *shame* about our bodies. Too often we're hobbled by a deeply entrenched self-disgust—and a terrible fear of anyone finding out the full extent of how physically imperfect and unacceptable we believe we really are.

A friend of mine I'll call Dan, who has three years of sobriety in AA, talks about his own experience in coming to this revelation, the revelation not only that he exists as a physical being but that accepting this means addressing the realities of his physical body, needs, hungers, and fears. "I didn't just drink," Dan says. "I'm in my early forties, old enough to have checked out in the psychedelic generation. I loved doing tequila, which everyone said was more like doing mescaline than getting drunk and then doing mescaline or LSD on top of it, just to make sure I tripped as well as got ripped on alcohol. The best part of it was the feeling that I could escape *me*. It was a spiritual thing, I kept trying to tell myself. I could sort of astrally project myself out of this earth-bound piece of flesh I had to drag around. Of course one of the reasons I wanted to get out of that flesh was that it was fat. I've been obese since I was a kid. Drugs and alcohol allowed me to float up and out of a body I'd learned, very early on, to loathe. I'm the classic last-kid-to-be-chosen-for-the-team. I can't tell you how bad other kids' taunting made me feel. Junior high and high school were one long nightmare. I hated everything about my body—how it looked, how it smelled, everything. It's like it had nothing to do with me. It was some punishment, something I had to be trapped in because I was bad. I was born bad—that was it. My body was some kind of punishment, a horrible life sentence. The only possible escape from all this self-hate was booze and drugs. And taking drugs to escape the world felt, somehow, with the encouragement you got from everybody during the hippie era, like the right thing to do: tune in and drop out. For me, that meant getting so zonked that I could literally forget I existed.''

In sobriety, Dan's biggest shock has been that he can't escape his ''hereness.'' ''Not that I haven't tried,'' he says. ''There isn't a Zen meditation class around here I haven't gone to. I'm always trying to get 'spiritual,' which I've begun to see is attached to my old desire to forget I'm a physical being. This was getting dangerous, too. Now that I didn't drink or drug anymore, I was taking to food with a new vengeance. I was gaining even more weight in sobriety. And it was having an effect on my health. My blood pressure was shooting way up. I was always tired. My answer was to get even more spiritual—look for new gurus, meditate more, seek new ways to check out, lose myself in some kind of out-of-body philosophy. It's only recently that I began to see how I was just trying to escape in some of the same old ways.''

Dan had a breakthrough about this recently when an old girlfriend came back into town and looked him up. ''I met Shirley in my last year of college when I was getting zonked but was still young enough, still just barely together enough to act halfway normal, get through the day. Shirley was different from anyone else I knew. She was never a part of the hard-core drug group that I was getting into. Sometimes she'd have a couple glasses of wine and maybe do a toke or two of pot, but she stopped because she said it made her dizzy and she didn't like the feeling. But she was different in other ways, too. She seemed to see something good in me. When I was around her, I didn't feel like a fat oaf. She could sort of get me to forget all the bad stuff I'd always believed about myself. We'd do things like go to movies. Okay, I'd have to smoke some dope and get reasonably tanked before going out. But, like I said, I could still act relatively normal. We'd go for coffee afterward, talk about stuff, like whatever the movie was about. Sometimes she'd tell me about her family. Her parents had escaped from Poland just before the Second World War: they were Jewish, and the stories she told about how they got out were hair-raising. Talking with Shirley, listening to her, was unique for me. She talked about the world outside us, something bigger than we were. When I was with her I saw life differently. Like there was more to it than I usually allowed myself to see. All I talked about with anyone else was drugs and getting wasted.''

Then, as Dan tells it, he blew it. "She invited me over for Thanksgiving dinner; it was just going to be the two of us. It was the most romantic thing we'd ever planned. And I guess that was what freaked me. I remember looking at myself in the mirror before going over. I'd really tried to look nice for her, even ironed a shirt! God, I'd never done that before. But all I could see was my fat face, my big belly. I started to hate myself. Why was Shirley putting up with me? Because she felt sorry for me? I started getting angry at her. I wasn't going to be anyone's patsy, anyone's charity case. I opened a bottle of tequila, started drinking it. I looked at the clock as I drank, the time got later and later, past the time I said I'd be over. The phone rang, I didn't answer it. I just drank more. I wasn't going to give Shirley the satisfaction of talking to her. I took out some hash, decided the best thing I could do was get really blitzed. Went through this long anger and self-pity trip. It was like I had to get out of myself any way I could. Thank God for mind-altering substances, I thought. It was either that or suicide.

"It got toward midnight, that's about the last thing I remember. That, and the one last time I looked at myself in the mirror, saw my ugly fat face and body and started to punch myself in the mouth. Hard. I actually broke the skin on my lip, started bleeding. It was almost a charge to do that to myself. I almost loved the pain. Then I must have passed out."

Dan woke up the next day with a horrendous hangover made worse by the "most sinking feeling of shame I'd ever felt up until then. I put it together, I really allowed myself to face for the moment that I'd ruined Shirley's holiday. She hadn't invited anyone over but me. I pictured the candles she would have lit, the food kept warm on the stove, and the minutes and hours ticking by. God, I thought, I can never talk to her again. That was the only option—I can't even *see* her again. And from that moment on, I hid. Didn't pick up the phone for three weeks. Made sure I wasn't anywhere near where I might bump into her. Then I got this card in the mail, just before Christmas. All it said, was, 'Why didn't you call? What's wrong?' and then her name. The shame came back full force, and I dealt with it in my usual way. I drank, smoked dope, got wasted, and hid.

"I managed to avoid her for a couple months after

the Thanksgiving mess. I just turned my back on her. God, I felt like a shit. But as usual, the way I dealt with that or any other feeling was simply to get wasted again. But now, after a hell I won't bore you with except to say that it just went down from there and it's a miracle I'm alive, I've worked my way into sobriety. I still don't always buy everything I hear in NA and AA, but the fellowship, the *people* caring about me, and the way I've begun to work the Twelve Steps have all simply changed my life. The two biggest changes are somehow linked: I don't hate myself as much, and I don't feel I'm alone." Dan pauses and sighs. "What *hasn't* changed is, I'm still fat."

Being fat wasn't his only problem. "My health went to hell the last ten years of drinking and drugging. I had severe intestinal cramps, my liver was swollen, my blood pressure was sky high, and my teeth were rotting. That's maybe the worst. I lost a few front teeth in my bottom jaw. After three years of sobriety, I'm only now investigating what I might be able to do about that—I'm starting to look into cheaper, non-profit dental clinics, that kind of thing, that my sponsor and other friends in recovery have recommended. But I haven't *done* anything about it yet. I'm just too scared, still too ashamed that I've let my mouth get this bad. Sometimes I'll find myself laughing at something in a meeting, I'll just lose myself in how funny it is, and then I'll remember my toothless smile and I'll shut my mouth. I still have such self-hate about this. It's like—well, my sponsor says, beware of the Two T's: teeth and taxes. For some reason, recovering alcoholics and addicts seem to be more frightened of their teeth and their taxes than just about anything else!''

Dan says that he was terrified of seeing Shirley again. ''I wanted to make amends to her. I wanted to do all that good program stuff—let her know how sorry I was I'd treated her so badly years before. But I couldn't bear for her to see me. All I could think of was my missing teeth, my fat belly and—oh yeah, my *very* thinning hair. She'd gotten my address from our college alumni office, she'd written me a letter saying she was going to be passing through the city I lived in and that she'd love to get together with me. It was like an electrical storm went through my brain when I got that letter. I wanted to see her so much, and I was so desperately afraid of seeing her, all at the same time. But, well, I'm in recovery now—I keep reminding myself of that. And I'm learning to face things in ways I never could before. I knew somehow that seeing Shirley again was essential to me—it had to do with my recovery, but it also had to do with wanting to see her because she'd been the only human being back then who cared about me. Truth was, I loved her. Even though I still felt so ugly—God, I almost broke out in hives the night before the day we were to meet—I knew I wanted to go through with it.''

Dan's eyes grow soft at the memory of seeing Shirley again for the first time. He laughs. ''I was like a nervous kid about to go on a first date. I'd tried to dress so carefully for her, I wore a dark shirt and black pants which I hoped would make me look thinner, I'd practiced smiling in a mirror without opening my mouth so she wouldn't see I was missing teeth, I doused myself with cologne, used this 'thickener' shampoo to make my hair look like I wasn't losing it. When I saw her come into the restaurant—we'd agreed to meet at this nice place for lunch (I'd picked it because the lights were low)—I felt both wonderful and terrible. She looked terrific. I looked—how? Terrible. At first I couldn't get past my own nervous self-hate. But then something helped me to relax, something in her eyes. It was simple: She was so happy to see me! I'd never *seen* anyone so happy to see me. It was like I remembered from years ago—she still saw something good in me, something that went beneath the surface. It was like she could look inside me, almost see my soul.''

Dan says it wasn't only his "soul" Shirley later told him she saw. "She kept going on about how good I looked—how healthy! When I began to tell her that I'd stopped drinking and taking drugs, she almost cried. 'That's it,' she said. 'I was so afraid for you back then. You were getting so pale—you just looked so physically sick all the time, and I knew it was all the stuff you were drinking and smoking and swallowing. But now, it's like you got a blood transfusion. You've got color! Even your eyes look different—brighter.' Then she really did cry. 'I was so afraid for you. And now—now, it's a miracle to see you so *here.*' ''

Dan says he knew right then what she was talking about. "It's not that I suddenly felt wonderful-looking. But I remember the first weeks I stopped drinking and drugging—well, I stopped drinking for a few months before I stopped smoking pot, so it came in stages. But even the first meetings I went to, I saw something different, something I wasn't used to. It bothered me, actually. Everyone there looked—how do I say this?

Awake. It was more than that nobody was nodding out. It was like there was some light that had been turned on inside them. Like Shirley said about me, they were *here*. And I began to get the inkling that while I'd gone on worrying about my weight and my teeth and my balding head, thinking that was all anyone could see, something else was happening, something my sobriety was taking care of without me even knowing it. It was like, I was just getting more and more alive. And that's really what people responded to—that's what I respond to in the people I like in the program. I began to think, who am I attracted to? Not just sexually. As friends. And I began to list my friends in recovery. When I thought about it, I could have found fault, I guess, in this or that physical detail. Too fat, too short, whatever. But I didn't even think about that. What I was really responding to went deeper than all that. And it was a kind of beauty.''

Dan laughs again. ''This took some time to put together. It's not like, bingo! Shirley tells me I look healthy and suddenly I'm full of high self-esteem. All I knew at that moment was that whatever it was that made Shirley happy to see me and me happy to see her had to do with something different than my weight, teeth, or hair. On her—I'd started to notice crows' feet! She did look a little older, after all. But did that make a difference? No. It really didn't. Which meant, maybe the stuff I obsessed over about my own appearance didn't have so much all-fired importance either.''

"It's something more than self-acceptance"

What Dan realized wasn't so much just that conventional notions of "beauty" weren't so important after all. "I'd still rather not be fat, and I wish my teeth were better and that I wasn't going bald," Dan says. "But what seeing Shirley again did for me was make me realize that I was *acceptable* even if I was fat, or missing a few teeth and some hair. Those imperfections didn't mean I was a monster! That was the biggest thing: I saw that maybe I could accept myself a little more as I was. That didn't mean I had to stay stuck where I was. But maybe I could get some clarity about what I might want to change, what I might have the power to change! Like, I could go to a dentist. I could start eating more reasonably. This was all in my power to do. I guess what happened is that I wasn't quite so afraid of thinking about my physical state, I could at least conceive of bringing it more out into the open. And it boiled down to a new kind of self-acceptance. Talking to my sponsor or anyone else about my teeth, for example, means accepting that they're a problem for me. It means admitting I need help. And whoa—here I go back again to the first moments of my sobriety.

"What helped me to get sober? It was the moment I realized I couldn't do it on my own. It was the moment I reached out for help. But I couldn't get to that moment, just like I couldn't get to the moment of walking into a dentist's office, unless I accepted—full, flat-out *accepted*—certain realities. My mouth is in bad shape.

I can't fix it on my own. I want to get it fixed. I need help to get it fixed.''

This has been a kind of light bulb to Dan, that the process which has worked to keep him sober could also apply to any other change he might want to bring about in his life. As Dan says about how he got sober, ''I started with discomfort—the pain of losing everything, of being half-dead as a drunk and an addict. And somehow, one day, that pain began to lead me, to help me break through my denial about what I was doing to myself. I realized, suddenly, '*Aha!* That's what I am— I'm a drunk and an addict.' The pain was still there, but now at least I was calling a spade a spade and it was a more specific pain. It was telling me something more than just that I hurt. 'I want to stop getting wasted,' is what that pain made me realize. 'I can't do it on my own,' is somehow what I also intuitively knew. 'So you need help,' my pain told me. And that's what got me to seek help—looking at my pain, then listening to it. But the important thing is, it didn't come from beating myself up for being a drunk. It came from *accepting* myself as a drunk. I had to *see* myself before it could become clear what I needed to *do* with myself.''

Dan says he knows this is a kind of magical key, one that seeing Shirley again helped him to appreciate on a deeper level. ''It's something more than self-acceptance. You know, back when I realized I was a drunk and an addict and I needed help, what I forget is that I must have thought I was *worth* helping, or I wouldn't have sought that help. In other words, somewhere deep inside me, I must have loved myself enough to get that help. I must have loved myself enough to care what happened to me!''

Dan says that realizing he was capable of loving himself, that in fact loving himself was central to how and why he's been able to get sober and how and why he might be able to address other painful realities about himself, doesn't come in an avalanche. ''The old self-hate is such a reflex. I know from my own sobriety that when I started to feel better, sleep better, start to get to work on time, all the stuff I couldn't do when I drank and drugged, it freaked me out. The good stuff is sometimes harder to deal with than the bad. Like my not being able to accept, all those years ago, that Shirley might actually *like* me. I'm uncomfortable with good feelings, with success. And my reflex is to slip right back into that old comfortable self-hate. Except it's not working so well anymore. I can't lie to myself like that. I *do* care what happens to me now. Sobriety has changed me, it's changed me without my even realizing the change was happening, like how Shirley could see my health even when I couldn't. I want better things for myself. I want to—look good! There's nothing wrong with that, is there? I can't stay in the dark for long anymore. I just keep getting back to wanting to grow again. Sometimes sobriety seems like a curse, the way it's always encouraging me to get out there and live!'' Dan laughs. ''But when I think of the alternative. . . .''

Not everyone is battling obesity, baldness, and bad teeth. But nearly every recovering addict and alcoholic I've listened to identifies with Dan's pain and self-hate and fear of ''exposure.'' The twenty-five-year-old marathon runner, not an ounce of extra fat on her, who's

battling anorexia as much as she's battling the urge to
go back to blocking out her fear of imperfection with
drugs and alcohol: on the face of it, she's got everything
anyone could want, what the world would call a "great
body," good health, beauty, youth. But inside, she's
battling many of the same demons Dan faced when he
got that long-ago glimpse of himself in a mirror and
responded to it by punching himself in the mouth. The
disease of addiction is merciless, heartless in the way
that it arises from and reinforces our fear and self-
hatred. Dan and other recovering friends of mine teach
me that when we start to hate our bodies, what we perceive to be our intolerable physical imperfections, we're
giving ourselves a red flag warning. As Dan puts it,
"I'm not really hating my fat ugly body. I'm hating
something deeper. I'm hating who I *am.*" That's the
real disease we're battling, and the real source of our
bodily disgust and shame.

How do you battle these negative, debilitating feelings most effectively? If Dan is right, a good start is to
remember what happened when you looked into your
heart and acknowledged that you were addicted, that
you were ill and needed help. More than needed it—
deserved it. All you have to do is remember, truly
re-experience the moment you surrendered to this re-
alization, a moment when, somehow, your self-hate gave
way to self-acceptance and, eventually, to something
even more miraculous and healing: self-love. It's okay
to be whoever you are when you allow yourself to enter
this oasis. But something more can happen: once you
feel and accept your essential "okayness," you often
find the resources to go a little further toward becoming

the person—even the *physical* person—you truly want to be.

"You don't need all your teeth to smile," Dan says, summing it up for himself. "But that doesn't mean I'm not calling a dentist."

Men's Feelings of Shame

Merle Fossum

*Merle Fossum is a husband, father, tree farmer,
outdoorsman, and writer. He is co-founder of the
Family Therapy Institute in St. Paul, Minnesota
where he is a family therapist.*

> *Being Human is difficult.*
> *Becoming human is a life-long process.*
> *To be truly human is a gift.*
> —ABRAHAM HESCHEL

He walked into my office and gave me the standard
greeting, "Hi, Merle, how are you?" But the tone of
his voice was more tense than usual. His eyes looked
like black marbles set in granite. As we sat down to
begin his weekly therapy session, he first gasped for
air, then let out a deep sigh, and said, "I need to tell
you something I've never told anyone before in my
life."

The moment for him had arrived to take the risk.
Still, he couldn't quite get it out. He stood on the brink
of a new reality in his life. Up to that moment, he had

total control over a secret that he had kept totally within himself. No one else in the world knew. Now, he was about to break and let one other person know. This shift from having no one else know to letting someone else know was a huge personal change.

I understood when he hesitated a moment there on the brink. He hemmed and hawed as if standing atop a high diving board. He said, "Maybe you won't think it's all that big a deal. I suppose you hear this kind of thing all the time."

My imagination was running miles ahead. I thought of a dozen terrible secrets a man might be carrying around. Did he kill somebody as a teenager? Has he been embezzling money from his company? Is he cheating on his wife?

Finally he blurted it out. "I'm hooked on pornography. I've been buying magazines with erotic pictures of women for years. I cut out my favorite pictures and save them in locked files at home. When I'm alone I go through them, I arrange and sort them as if they were my private harem. I can lose hour after hour in fantasies with those pictures. I often masturbate with them. I've tried to throw them all out, but I can't. It feels like I'm throwing away my best friends. I've always told myself that this doesn't hurt anybody, but I'm not so sure anymore. I don't think my wife knows anything about this, but it makes me feel like a total scumbag after I waste half a day in a secret fantasy. It makes me depressed. My wife knows I get depressed, but she doesn't know why. I tell her I don't know why either, but that's a lie. I've promised myself a thousand times I'll never buy another magazine, but suddenly on my lunch break,

there I am again, in a sleazy bookstore buying another
one.''

Defining Shame and Guilt

The man with his secret was awash in shame. *Guilt*
and *shame* are often used as words with the same meaning. But I've learned in my psychotherapy practice and
my personal life that big doors open for people in their
growth when they understand the important difference
between the two words.

Shame is feeling hopelessly awful about yourself as
a person. A shameful man may say these sorts of things
to himself: *I am less than other people. As a person,
as a man, at my core, I'm not good enough, or I'm not
smart enough, or I'm bad, or inadequate, or ugly. If
other people* really *knew me, they wouldn't like me. I
can make no honest bridge to others. I must find ways
to relate that don't rely on honesty. I can only have
friends if I put on a good face or charm them and hide
the deeper unfinished, chaotic parts of myself.*

Guilt, on the other hand, is a painful feeling about
my actions, not my worth as a person. It's knowing I'm
just like everyone else in my imperfection and incom-
pleteness. It's regretting having made a mistake or having done something that violated my values. It's
knowing that my behaviors have consequences, and
that I feel badly about them when they hurt others or
myself.

For example, I feel guilty about thoughtlessly forget-
ting to meet a friend for lunch after setting the appoint-
ment with him. I know he arranged his schedule to be

there as we agreed, and then he sat alone waiting for me and I never showed up. That doesn't mean I'm a bad person; it means I made a mistake. I feel guilty when, opening a door, I bump a little child on the opposite side and knock her down. It hurts me to know my actions hurt a child, even if it was unintentional. Guilt is being in tune with my impact on others. No one can be an active, caring person without feeling guilt at times. It's a healthy, human feeling.

Shame is about myself as a person. Guilt is about my behavior. With guilt, I keep my self-respect. Out of the pain of guilt, I try to find a way to make repairs—to make things right again. But no repair is possible from the perspective of shame. Shame destroys my self-respect and dignity. There is no fixing it up, no repair, no way back. It leads to no personal growth. The only responses to shame are to cover up, hide, or run away. Sometimes people cover their shame by putting on a very smooth, perfect exterior, and by keeping secrets. Sometimes they run away by simply disappearing from friendships.

Shame Is More Than Low Self-Esteem

Early in my career as a family therapist, I spent nine months with a great teacher, Virginia Satir, in a small, intensive family therapy training program in Palo Alto, California. My work with her changed my life both personally and professionally. Her central theme for our group was this: *self-esteem is the main issue in emotional well-being*. We examined self-esteem as it develops in small children, and we worked to improve impaired self-esteem in children with problems. We worked with couples and saw how their relationships were troubled because of low self-esteem. We studied the self-esteem factors in good and bad communication. Virginia's definition of high self-esteem went like this: *high self-esteem is when my image of myself matches my image of how I should be.*

Years after my intensive training with her, I learned more about alcoholism. It is a disease often carried within the family from one generation to the next. In a similar way, the abused child of one generation may be the abusive parent in the next. Observing these generational patterns with my own eyes again and again had a great impact on me. We can work in therapy on self-esteem; people can have powerful successes in their careers and esteem-building experiences with friends, but still they return again and again like migrating swallows, even against their conscious will, to the same self-destructive patterns of prior generations. The great theoretical question in the field of family therapy has moved from, "How can we promote change?" to "Why do things stay so much the same?"

What Virginia Satir taught about self-esteem was my beginning point, my base to build on as I grew professionally. At first, I had thought of self-esteem almost as if we each had a thermometer by which we could gauge higher or lower self-esteem. I didn't see that its opposite, self-hate or shame, has its own momentum apart from self-esteem. I don't recall how or when the concept of shame as a psychological term came into my field of view. I know that other therapist colleagues were interested in it, too, and we learned from each other.

My friend and colleague, Dr. Marilyn J. Mason, and I worked as co-therapists with several families, and several ideas about shame as a hidden dynamic in family relations developed out of our work.

One important idea I learned shows how the dynamics of self-hate work—that shame begets more shame. It is not just a low reading on the thermometer of self-esteem. Shame is something like cancer—it grows on its own momentum. Positive self-esteem experiences don't fully overcome the negative corrosion of shame unless a person faces it directly.

The man who compulsively shamed himself by immersion in pornography ritually degraded himself. He revitalized his shame feelings over and over again with his actions, just as the father who reenacts the abuse his father wrought on him does when he abuses his child. No amount of friends, no amount of job success or marital happiness, or other positive experiences, as helpful and encouraging as they are, will block the cancer of self-defeating behavior in these men until they confront their shame directly. To focus on the moral questions of pornography doesn't help him because it isn't a guilt problem; it's a shame problem. Finding acceptable images for him to view or helping him feel better about what he is doing doesn't touch the heart of his problem. Regardless of the behavior, men burdened by shame first need to stop the behavior that actively revitalizes their shame, and then they need to face their underlying shame issues.

What Are Men Ashamed Of?

The experience of shame, whether male or female, comes out of a feeling that our humanness is diminished, that we don't fully qualify as members of the human community, that we aren't good enough to be accepted and loved as we are. Shame transcends gender. The waste and hurt is as bad for either sex. Yet, it seems different things trigger shame responses in men than in women.

Weakness

For example, problems that show weakness might bring up shame in men. Most men automatically think they ought to deal with their problems alone and be cool and unfeeling about them. A job problem, a health problem, or a family problem can bring feelings of weakness. Naturally, these problems come along for everyone as part of life. So men cannot avoid shame unless they find other ways of coping besides expecting to be strong and stoically "toughing it out."

In contrast, women in our culture are far more accepting of weakness. Of course, it feels good to be strong, but vulnerability doesn't raise doubts about a woman's femininity. When a problem comes along, women are more comfortable telling friends what is going on, and maybe crying together about it. Women don't have the self-esteem barrier to cross before accepting help. This flexibility gives them stronger coping methods for dealing with the normal life set-backs and crises that can't be avoided.

Body Image

Both men and women are highly subject to shame about body issues. Anyone with a scar, a birthmark, even a bruise knows the power of body image to trigger shame. Physical disabilities can pose profound challenges to a person's self-respect, not because there is anything shameful about them, but because they challenge a person to answer, "My dignity has nothing to do with my physical image or strength."

Sexual Performance

It seems to me that men are especially subject to shame about sex and sexual performance. If a man's sexual performance isn't satisfactory to his mate, he is likely to feel shameful and want to hide the fact. We live in a culture that tells men to be the sexual sophisticates. That is a hurtful myth because it doesn't match the reality at least half of the time. When a man doesn't fulfill the sophisticate image, he may feel he is less of a man. Any problem with sex in a relationship may feel like *his* responsibility and a sign of failure.

Providing for Family

The good provider image is a big one for men. When this image is not fulfilled, either because of limited opportunity to work, lack of skills, or job loss due to economic changes, a man's shame can be triggered. When a man has job problems, he can be under just as much stress from the shame as from the financial pressure. He thinks he should be in control. If a man isn't meeting his father's goals for him in a career or isn't achieving as much out in the world as his father did, he may feel like a failure.

Shame and Our Fathers

To move psychologically out of childhood into adulthood, a man must transpose his father's standards and goals for him into a new version that fits him. If he never got complete acceptance and approval from his dad, he may stay focused on a deep feeling that something is wrong with him. If he never got beyond anger and rebellion against what his dad stood for, his emancipation remains incomplete, and he may carry shame until he can let go of that anger. Facing shame and healing from it means respecting ourselves. For many of us, that means coming to terms with our fathers and making peace with them.

Seeing our fathers as separate people on their own life journey, just as we are on our life journey, and accepting our fathers allows us to accept ourselves. When we can deal with our fathers in the flesh, it helps us get beyond those shame and emancipation hurdles. Childhood images of our fathers may have been bigger than life, seeing them as either a hero or a devil. As adults, our images don't mature without person-to-person experience in learning to know the real man. He has thoughts and feelings, doubts and imperfect choices. Knowing him within the same human dimensions that we live our own lives and still respecting him creates a base for our own self-respect. Other men help, too, and they can serve as a stand-in for our father if he isn't available.

Facing Hardships

Many men believe the most admirable trait is to endure hardship without flinching. But this trait makes them so rigid it can create a blindness to the reality of their own feelings. Thus, they become less adaptable to change. I remember one instance when that belief was reinforced in my life. It made me very angry. It was at my grandmother's funeral. My father's mother died at the age of ninety-one; my father was sixty-eight years old. After the funeral service a few tears rolled down his cheeks. The pastor noticed them and I suspect he intended to bolster Dad by challenging him to recapture his stoic facade. His response to Dad's tears was, "Leif, I always thought you were stronger than that!" I was furious at the pastor because my father had the right to feel grief at his mother's death. I was also proud of my father for his integrity and honesty in feeling his grief and feeling his attachment to his mother.

Having feelings, and releasing our control to face them as they are, takes courage and is more dignified than squelching them. Hiding and stuffing our feelings may give the external appearance of control and strength, but experiencing them makes us more genuinely strong and flexible for coping with life and moving on.

The "Male Ego"

The *male ego* is a term I hear women use. Sometimes it's called the *fragile male ego*. What I think they are talking about is a man's susceptibility to shame. I think women see something about us that we don't see ourselves. We can learn from them if we listen.

Women tell us that many of them have taken on the job of propping men up, helping maintain a man's image of strength and power, being careful not to challenge men so strongly that their weak spots get exposed. This seems to be women's awareness of men's shame. They tell us they've learned that if certain buttons get pushed, a man gets defensive, angry, shameful, or he goes away. Women are naturally quite ambivalent about the whole thing. On one hand, they try to treat men gently because they don't want to be hurtful or abandoned; on the other hand, they're angry about maintaining this charade instead of having a more intimate relationship. Sometimes women laugh about this thing they see in men because it looks so silly from the outside.

As a man grows in recovery, he learns that his buttons, his weak spots, belong to himself. How he feels is not the fault of someone who pushed his buttons. He takes on his own feelings and deals with the discomfort without shame. He doesn't expect his wife or lover to play the role of Weak Violet or the Dumb Blond to make him look stronger and smarter.

Wading Through the Stream of Shame

To understand the sources of shame, think of all of your daily activities as a giant landscape. You have your work, your friends and family relationships, meals, money management, home and car maintenance. Now, imagine an expanse that you wander through containing hills and buildings, trees, roads, and rivers. Each feature in this landscape represents a part of your life. Some features are very prominent because they represent activities you spend a great deal of time with, while others are far back in a corner you see only occasionally.

Imagine that from time to time as you wander your landscape of daily activity, you suddenly plunge into the stream of shame. Sometimes you see it coming. Sometimes it happens without warning; you just end up in the water with all your clothes on. No matter how you got there, it always feels cold and dirty and smells bad.

Most people have no awareness that they are actually landing in the same stream every time. The fact that you stumble on a shame event today when your boss asks you a question is directly connected to the fact that you learned the shame response in your past. It is a stream that has a source or several sources. The original source of your stream of shame may not be in view anymore, but it exists. If you become more acquainted with your stream, you won't have to be such a victim of it or go swimming in it quite as often.

Traumatic Origin of Shame

The traumatic origin of shame is the specific experience in your life of being treated badly and having your dignity or innocence stolen from you. This includes all the ways that you may have been put down, abused, made a scapegoat, ridiculed, blamed, used, or neglected. These experiences leave scars. People often don't remember the events, but these events taught them how to feel unworthy. Or, they do remember them, but they discount the events because they insist they're not affected by them.

Bad treatment of boys often gets dismissed as toughening them up for manhood. The scars that form the lifelong stream of shame for adult men are too often dismissed and ignored. Trying to create an image of toughness and covering memories of the abuse and the shame it instilled, is one of the ways development of genuine masculine strength gets stifled.

If we are treated inhumanely, we feel degraded and ashamed. Something has been stolen from us—our dignity. Such abuse can be more devastating for children than for adults because children don't understand what is happening. When a child is brutalized or is quietly treated badly, he may not even know that it is wrong or unfair. Still, his dignity is stolen and shame quickly becomes part of his identity.

We can see how this happens most clearly in a victim of an ordeal like a serious car accident, a fire, a mugging, or a hostage crisis. The fallout from the trauma goes on for a long time after the event is over. The victim can become extremely nervous, sleepless, and tortured with self-doubt and inadequacy long after the event, even though the victim was in no way to blame. Ongoing abuse has a similar impact but may not be as easy to identify as one big terrible event.

Inherited Generational Origin of Shame

Inherited generational origins of shame first became known to me in my work with adults who could find no traumatic incidents in their own history. Yet they had all the vulnerability to shame that victims of traumatic shaming have. When we looked, we found shaming events in prior generations. For example, the father of a client was abandoned by his parents at the age of ten. It was a family secret that felt too awful for the father to tell his son about until the son came asking questions. The stream of shame flowed, not just in the lifetime of my client, but from a source in a previous generation unknown to him, into his own present experience.

The mother of one deeply shameful client was the childhood victim of incest. Other clients came from generations of brutal, abusive racism and anti-Semitism. Basic human dignity was stolen from their parents, grandparents, and great-grandparents, and the shame response, once seeded in the family's emotional climate, was active in a man's present life. In the inherited shame process, families adopt rules of behavior that are meant to defend them against shame. But in reality, the rules of behavior hide the shame and allow it to be passed unwittingly from generation to generation.

Eight Rules of the Shame-Bound Family

Rule number one: Be in control at all times. *

This rule leads people in a family to control themselves and to keep everyone predictable. It squelches spontaneity because people are afraid if they are spontaneous they'll get abused and look bad to other family members. Many family members become extremely manipulative as they try to follow this rule. Some gain control by being domineering, others by being ill, and still others by being sweet and pleasing.

Rule number two: Always be right, do the right thing.

We call this "the perfection rule" because it doesn't allow room for the natural human process of making mistakes and learning from experience. The humanness of imperfection is squelched by this rule. Everyone is imperfect so people feel a little less honest with themselves as they try to follow it. Either they get so good at it that they cover their shame with self-righteousness, or they have a feeling of failure because only the impossible (perfection) is acceptable.

*F.R. Ford and J. Herrick "Family Rules/Family Life Styles." *American Journal of Orthopsychiatry.* Vol. 44 (1974): 61-69.

Rule number three: If something doesn't happen as planned, blame someone, yourself or another person. *

With this rule, surprise or puzzlement is almost always cause for attaching blame. "If you were different, I could be happy." "Why do you always have your foot in my way?" "If I hadn't talked about the weather, we would have had a sunny day." "It's your fault that I put my fist through the wall because you made me angry." These are examples of things that might be said in a family that lives by this rule.

Rule number four: Deny feelings, especially the negative or vulnerable ones like anxiety, fear, loneliness, grief, rejection, or need.

I've sat with families who follow this rule, and, as I got acquainted with them, I began to feel a deep sense of underlying loneliness or sadness in their stories. I could even see those feelings show in their faces. But when I told them about it they were totally unaware of the feelings themselves. They said, "Oh no, you don't understand. We don't feel that way at all," and they were not consciously lying. They actually didn't know what they felt. So these families are never able to share feelings because they can't admit them.

*F.R. Ford and J. Herrick "Family Rules/Family Life Styles." *American Journal of Orthopsychiatry.* Vol. 44 (1974): 61-69.

Rule number five: Don't expect reliability or constancy in relationships.

We found wide variations in the quality of contact between people in these families, with little consistency from one encounter to the next. One time a couple may be like a pair of lovebirds, and the next day, for no apparent reason, one will withdraw, creating great emotional distance. Or they may have an intense crisis over a conflict and, without ever resolving anything, they somehow put the problem aside and carry on as if nothing had ever happened. These families need an outside person, such as a therapist, to ask the question: "How did you get from point A to point B?" They often answer something like, "I don't know. It didn't seem important." In fact, they probably feel the abrupt switches and psychological disappearances are normal. It is therapeutic for them to look at transitions and question the process of mood swings within their family system.

Rule number six: Don't bring transactions or disagreements to completion or resolution.

With this rule, people living with shame, covering secrets, or hiding from themselves are fearful of reaching conclusions. Some are deeply afraid of conflict, so they flee from it. They don't realize that if you don't engage in some conflict, you can never resolve anything. Then differences just get stored up and accumulate in an underlying tension between otherwise loving people. Some may be frightened of being held accountable or blamed for the decisions they make. Others may be simply continuing what they learned to do as children with no greater reasons for doing it than it's the only way they know.

Rule number seven: Don't talk openly and directly about shameful, abusive, or compulsive behavior in our family.

I first became acquainted with this pattern in families with alcoholism and other drug addiction. It's often true that the neighbors know before family members that someone's drug use is out of control. Family members feel deeply blocked from talking about it: they can't put their heads together to figure out what is going on. Adults who were sexually abused as children may have specific memories of the abusive experiences and yet wonder if they were abused or not. Since it was never acknowledged, they really don't know how to understand it.

Rule number eight: When disrespectful, shameful, abusive, or compulsive behavior occurs, disqualify it, deny it, or disguise it.

No one following this rule would say, "Grandpa Ben is alcoholic." They might say, "He has a little too much to drink once in a while." In another family, the abused child is blamed for provoking the parent's rage, rather than the parent admitting directly that he or she lost control in punishing the child. Abuse gets laughed at as if it were one of the family jokes. Overeating may be explained as a healthy appetite.

These eight rules describe a pattern of relationships, and yet every family is different and many of these rules overlap. If you see yourself and your family communication in any of these rules, you have something to put your finger on. They are ways that shame gets perpetuated in your life. It gets passed on to your children in the same ways. No one can change their family rules simply by saying, "Now I see it and I won't do that anymore." It's never that easy. Yet, knowing it, naming it, and having a label for it makes it different already. It gives you a handle you can grasp; then it's something you can work on. You no longer have to be in the dark or mystified by falling into the stream of shame. You no longer need to believe you alone deserve to be ashamed, because now you've got ways to understand its true source. Over time, with attention to the pattern, and with help, you will change.

Maintained Shame

The source of shame called maintained shame was exemplified at the opening of this chapter by the man addicted to pornography. It refers to any action or behavior a person engages in, often for pleasure, that has the side effect of abusing his self. Sometimes the loss of control is degrading; sometimes the invasion of boundaries is disrespectful; sometimes the violation of one's fundamental values is so great that the shame response is inevitable. In maintained shame, the repetition of actions that degrade one's self is the crucial factor. Anyone with an addictive or compulsive behavior is probably maintaining his shame and may not even know it.

The Shame-Rage Connection

Gershen Kaufman, the author of *Shame: The Power of Caring,* identified the way in which intense anger or rage can serve as a cover for shame.* He wrote that a person who flies into rage may feel suddenly exposed or in danger of looking like a fool. I think it's a common connection for men who have problems with anger attacks. They may never know that their underlying shame or self-hate was tapped. The only thing that shows on the outside is a sudden, uncontrollable, and even abusive rage.

An Example of Shame Covered by Rage

I have a friend who has a long-standing relationship with some fishing buddies. This group has been together for about fifteen years, and they go on fishing trips to Canada twice a year. Between trips they get together in twos and threes for lunch when they can and for an occasional evening out with their wives. These men know each other very well.

One spring, one of the men, Jed, began to act very moody and distant. The guys talked about him because they couldn't understand what was going on. The gossip in the community was spreading that Jed was doing a

---

*Gershen Kaufman, *Shame: The Power of Caring* (Cambridge, Mass.: Shenkman Press, 1980).

lot of gambling and was in deep financial trouble. But he never told his friends about it. So they decided the best way to be good friends was to talk directly to him. They decided to do that the following Wednesday when they were to meet and plan for the upcoming fishing opener.

His closest friend in the group, Bill, began by saying he had heard some things from his neighbor and wanted to hear straight from Jed what was going on. Jed instantly flew into anger. His face turned red with rage as he yelled that Bill was an S.O.B. and accused him of spreading malicious rumors. Everyone sat in silent shock at the intensity of Jed's attack. When he quit yelling, Jed stormed out of the house, didn't go on the fishing trip, and refused to talk to anyone in the group for weeks afterward.

The friends all felt abused by his rage and misunderstood. They vaguely wondered if they had done it wrong. Yet, they were sure that Jed's anger was abusive and out of bounds. This was a clear example of underlying shame that was covered by rage. Sadly, Jed's shame got perpetuated by his outburst and by his cutting off of the friendships, so no repair or resolution could be made.

The Shame–Self-Righteousness Connection

As we studied family systems that have a problem with shame, we usually found one or more members of the family who felt pious, better than others, unrealistically self-satisfied, or grandiose. These individuals seemed to be unaware of their own feelings of shame, but they lived in a family system where others felt very shameful. These self-righteous people are often critical; they say they hold high standards, and in many ways are quite successful in controlling their behavior. But they are unhappy and may not have close relationships with anyone. They are not aware of their motivations, and they don't realize how much their self-righteousness comes from a symbiotic relationship with the less-successful, less-powerful family members.

For example, a husband may be always critical of his wife. She accepts it and feels inadequate until one day he suddenly dies of a heart attack. Following her grief, she comes into her own. She no longer is loaning him her strength and self-respect by being one down to make him feel strong. She becomes a much more effective person. No one ever knew he was depending on her to feel good about himself. His self-righteousness was really covering his underlying feelings of shame. He had the same stolen dignity and pain that other shameful people have, but it was hidden by a life pattern of control and arrogant self-righteousness. Neither he nor she could grow out of their shame until that symbiotic pattern was broken, either by greater honesty or by death.

Recovery from Shame

Of all my work with men and women in therapy, to walk the path with a client out of shame into self-respect is the most rewarding experience. That walk is as awesome as any wilderness experience I have ever had with towering mountain walls and raging waterfalls, and as tender as a healing stream in warm sunshine. A man's confrontation with his personal, private human core is profound. Facing our shame teaches us what true humanity is. We all have shame to face within ourselves because we all have been treated badly in one way or another and felt diminished. We all have violated ourselves in some way. We all are bombarded daily by depersonalizing messages. The rampant racism, sexism, materialism, drug orientation, and militarism around us diminishes our value as individuals. These evil forces cause human beings to be treated like objects and undermine our self-respect. So, if you feel you have work to do, you are not alone. We all have a lifelong task of becoming truly human rather than settling for indignity and shame.

Maxwell Maltz is quoted as saying, "You must fight off a 'bad luck' way of thinking as if you were dealing with an invasion of hostile forces—for that is precisely what you are dealing with." After you become aware of your shame feelings, the next thing to do for your recovery is to make a solemn vow. Promise that you will no longer give your energy to hostility against yourself, to self-derogatory or self-hating purposes. Make a conscious decision to be on your own side, because there are enough harmful forces and events coming from outside yourself that would abuse you, put you down, or hurt you. Naturally, making the vow doesn't mean you can suddenly, willfully change. But it sets a standard for you to imperfectly adhere to, and keep returning to.

Many men are naive and they say, "I have no enemies!" These men are certain to get hurt. You need to know you have enemies; identify who and what they are, and be certain not to join their side. Your enemies include the depersonalizing forces just mentioned and those family rules that instill and perpetuate your shame. They also include inner attitudes of self-hate and hopelessness, and any people who diminish your recovery, strength, and health. You join your enemies when you mope around, mentally criticizing your basic nature. Your solemn promise means that you no longer berate yourself for your mistakes or indulge in the habit of calling yourself shameful or gutter names when you feel low. Leave that activity to your enemies. You can make mistakes. You can feel sad or ashamed. That's human. But, you begin the road out of shame by using your conscious mind and your will to befriend yourself. You consciously say the things to yourself that you would say to a dear, respected friend. "God loves you. You are a child of the universe. You deserve a place here like everyone else. You have a right to make mistakes." Another phrase my mother often used was, "It takes all kinds of people to make a world." Claim it as your right to be one kind of a person in a varied world!

Barriers to Recovery from Shame

Break down the alienation and invisible barriers between you and other people. You can do this in concrete and practical ways. For instance, have no secrets that aren't shared with someone. Everyone needs at least two or three people who know them very well. Certainly, some things you have to say won't make you look good, but with a trusted friend you don't always have to look good. Only a statue can be perfect, and even then it casts a shadow. Say to yourself, *I don't want to be a cold, lifeless statue. I want to be alive, a thriving human being with passion and feeling*. So let down your control over what your friends know. Let a few people know you as you are. As you let another person know you, you also get to know yourself. Expect your friends to accept you as you are.

Not Telling the Whole Story

It is also possible to keep up a barrier by telling only parts of your story to a person and telling other parts to someone else. Then you can say that you have told everything to someone. Still, no one person has all the pieces. No one really knows you totally, and you continue to feel vaguely mistrustful and alone, and your shame is preserved.

How Therapy Can Help

Sometimes taking down all barriers begins with help from a therapist. It is a safe place to let go of all private memories, thoughts, and feelings and to get a therapist's reactions. But therapy alone isn't enough. You must take that honesty outside the setting of the therapist's office and risk letting a trusted few know you with nothing held back. This kind of relationship builds over time; it doesn't suddenly happen in one conversation. When it does happen, you can have the elation and release of knowing you are accepted by others who really know you.

Leaving Relationships

Some of the shame a man feels may get perpetuated by simply disappearing from his relationships. Perhaps he has a friendship he cares about; then one day tension develops between him and his friend. Maybe he did something he feels badly about, or his friend did something he's mad about. The shameful response is to simply drop the relationship. No explanation, he just drops out of contact. Within families, people who grew up together—brothers, sisters, parents—may stop talking for years. The noted family therapist Murray Bowen studied these cut-offs within families, and he found that they prevent people from maturing and becoming strong individuals.

Disappearing from relationships is like taking a bunch of freshly picked string beans, blanching them, and sticking them in the freezer. All growth and change stops abruptly. Six months later you take them out of the freezer, and they're almost like the day you picked them. That's what we want with string beans but not with our lives. When a twenty-year-old man is thinking like a twenty-year-old, he is emotionally healthy and alive. But, when a thirty-year-old still thinks like a twenty-year-old, he has missed ten years of personal development and growth. Cutting off relationships, disappearing from them, refusing to talk or even to say good-bye, freezes a man's shame. It saves a man from having to deal with it head-on, but it also preserves it within him until it is dealt with honestly.

If you have old friends that once meant a lot to you and you abruptly dropped the relationship, or if you have parents, brothers, or sisters you've stopped all meaningful contact with, rid yourself of shame by contacting them. If this is going to work, you must do it with empathy for the other person. In some situations more harm is done by making contact, and silence is the most considerate choice. But in most cases, reestablishing contact, with a willingness to make apologies when necessary, is like a long-awaited homecoming. That's how shame can flow normally out of your life rather than storing it up in your mind.

Humility and Shame Are Two Different Traits

I used to think humility was the paradoxical virtue of being good because you thought you were bad. I thought it was almost the same as shame. But I've had several good talks about it with my male friends. It has become clear that humility is not the same as shame at all. In fact, shame and humility do not coexist in the same person. Humility is when a man with self-respect knows he has a place and a relationship with other people, with the world, with the cosmos, with the flow of time through the centuries. Humility is when a man doesn't presume to inflate, diminish, or in any way manipulate the image of where he fits in. Humility is to accept a leadership role and success for what it is when it comes, and to accept defeat with the same attitude.

From this truly humble perspective, we know we are more similar than different from others. We are the tiniest speck of dust in the infinite universe, with a lifetime as brief as a flash compared to the flow of billions of years of creation. Yet, the most admirable story is one where a person overcomes the obstacles to his dignity to make progress in the face of great difficulty, or when someone performs heroic acts of looking out for another person. Life is a risk for anyone who loves and cares about others and who tries to grow. If you say, "But it's so hard!" my reply is, "Yes, of course it is hard. But there is no alternative except stagnation or death. So why not get into the act and enjoy it?"

Exercises for Facing Your Shame

- What memories do you have of feeling that your dignity as a person was ridiculed or stripped away? How did you recover from that? Or are you still living with that indignity as if it has power over you? You can begin the healing of these memories by talking to someone about them.

- Do you have old friends or family members who once were important to you, but you have not contacted? Consider what it would take for you to bridge that gap. Would it be healing to write a letter and make amends? Would a telephone call be worth a risk to repair your shame? If you do this, it's best to talk to someone else about it beforehand to get his or her advice about it.

- Can you name any ways that you are habitually maintaining your shame? Were there some ways in your past that are not present today?

- If you give the entire job of opposing your enemies

to your enemies, you are free to put your whole self into being healthy, successful, and self-accepting. Write three sentences of support that an honest friend might say to you.

Healing
Shame-Based Spirituality

Ruth Schweitzer-Mordecai

Ruth Schweitzer-Mordecai, M.F.C.C., is a licensed psychotherapist. She has a private practice in Marin County, California, and specializes in addictions and spiritual issues. She is co-director of The New Genesis Center for Spiritual Growth and conducts retreats and workshops in the San Francisco Bay area on topics combining psychology and spirituality.

Discovering a Higher Power Who Wants Us to Be Free

Religion turns me off. All I ever felt in church was guilty. How can I turn myself over to the care of God when God just makes me feel bad about myself?

I've come to see, in recovery, that my parents used the idea of God to control me and make me "be good." Now it's hard to imagine a God who wants me to be free.

Recovery in Twelve Step programs is based on a spiritual awakening, as well as a belief in and reliance on

a Higher Power. Just as we learned how to have relationships with people in our family, we also learned
how to have a relationship with a Higher Power.

But what if, in seeking our spiritual awakening, we
find that our concept of God or a Higher Power came
from a spiritual system as dysfunctional as our addictive
family system? What if our spirituality is based on
shame? How can we free ourselves to uncover and trust
in a source that is not a continuation of our disease, but
is rather a guide and supporter of our recovery?

God—A Word with History

In the Third Step, we make a decision to turn our
will and our lives over to God, *as we understand
God*. But for many of us, *God* is a word with history.
We grew up learning about God—from our family,
our culture, our church or temple, our friends, or
other cultures. We may have developed a relationship
of our own with God, or we observed the relationships of others with a Higher Power. We knew of or
had relationships with people who represented the in-
stitutional church to us—ministers, priests, nuns, or
rabbis. All these things have had their impact on our
freedom to define a Higher Power for ourselves, and
by their nature, some of them may have created feelings of shame in us.

Unhealthy or Shame-Based Spirituality

There are different kinds of shame, from healthy to unhealthy. This unhealthy shame is like a wound we may think we cannot heal, an irreparable defect. For if we identify with our shame and believe we are defective, we can never develop full self-love. We will develop, instead, a false self to protect our shamed inner core. A false self cannot connect with a Higher Power. Only by being authentic with our wounds and wholeness can we make that connection.

Is Our Relationship with Our Higher Power Shame-Based?

We need to pay attention to how our concepts of a Higher Power cause us to feel about ourselves. Do they enhance our self-image, or cause us to see ourselves as an unworthy or lesser person?

I learned some time ago to also use this question to help me look at my relationships. I ask not only how I feel about a person, but also *how I feel about myself* when and after I am with that person. If my sense of self-worth is lower, something is wrong. Although I am responsible for my thoughts about myself, I am affected by those around me. I need to evaluate the benefits of a relationship in which it is difficult to feel okay about myself.

I find the same is true about my concept of a Higher Power. One negative spiritual approach I learned in childhood is what a friend of mine in seminary calls *worm theology*: God is all-wonderful and I am basically just a worm, a sinner. With an idea like this, we consider ourselves unworthy of God. To see ourselves as having a basically evil nature that we must constantly struggle against makes a healthy sense of self-worth difficult, if not impossible. This creates humiliation, which ensures we never feel proud or even good about who we are.

Pride often has bad press in recovery programs. But I think that a "Look, Ma, no hands" kind of need for recognition of our accomplishments is quite healthy and is not the pride of denial. This healthy recognition may be unavailable to us if we grew up with a critical parent and internalized this critical voice. So we are likely to be at home with our idea that God is a critical parent.

On Earning Acceptance

If we weren't adequately nurtured, it is hard to imagine receiving acceptance, so we keep trying to earn it. But true acceptance doesn't need to be earned. For instance, can you think of a time when you really blew it—were at your worst—and someone still managed to see the good in you? Perhaps even to see the pain inside you that was causing the negative behavior? That is what it's like to be truly accepted—accepted at our worst. This does not mean being supported in the unhealthy behavior, but being supported in spite of it.

Barriers to Healthy Spirituality

We cannot come to believe that a power greater than ourselves can restore us to sanity (wholeness), as described in Step Two of the Twelve Step programs, unless we can believe in a power whose *authority* is love *for* us, rather than power *over* us. We need a God who is always in our corner. Otherwise, we simply have another Parent, with a capital *P*, to please.

Neurotic guilt can also be a barrier to healthy spirituality. Such guilt has its roots in perfectionism. If I believe that God expects me to be perfect, I am setting a goal I will never achieve. I will continually feel guilty and not good enough for my Higher Power.

Yet, at times, our conscience is important. Then our struggle is to recognize and acknowledge when we have done things that are genuinely against our personal values. But genuine sorrow for wrongdoing brings sadness as well as guilt. We regret the action, not that we exist. Regretting our action doesn't bring anxiety, but rather a desire to change.

One More Set of Rules

If we are the child of a dysfunctional family, we may have had to be different from our real self to survive. We filled our emptiness inside with rules and values we picked up from others. We have not yet discovered our own values, so we assume roles and identities that are not really us. Then we feel guilty if we mess up by slipping out of these roles. We aren't in touch with our real needs and so depend on others for guidance.

For example, we may have learned that it is never okay to be angry, that we should turn the other cheek. Then we may feel guilty whenever we are angry. We try to repress it, but eventually we blow up and yell at our children, spouse, or the dog. But the guilt we feel is for breaking a rule that is not really ours.

If we believe our Higher Power wants us to obey the rules and prove that we are worthy, recovery can be just one more set of rules to judge ourselves by. It is not unusual, and can even be helpful, in early recovery to follow new rules. Eventually, however, growth in a recovery program brings us to the stage where we need to discover our own path and our own relationship with a Higher Power. If we can believe in a Higher Power who believes in us and welcomes our initiative and our unique gifts, even if they conflict with old rules, we can feel welcome in the universe. Then we are free to discover hidden talents and passions and use our creativity.

Clarifying Our View of a Higher Power

Many of us grew up with an overemphasized image of God as a *Father*. This can be the source of an idea that men are made in God's image but women are not. Some women have great difficulty recognizing the presence of God within themselves and may see men as somehow closer to God.

Also, both women and men often connect the image of Father God with their human father. If this is the only image, it results in a limited God, even in people who have had a healthy relationship with their fathers. If we conceive of God as Mother/Father, it can still keep us a child who never grows up spiritually. As anyone with time in recovery knows, growing up and assuming responsibility for our life isn't easy or comfortable. Seeing our Higher Power only as a parent can create a resistance to growth into adulthood.

There is also a way of being a child that keeps us hiding from reality. If we see God as a protector from the usual difficulties of life, we have found a retreat, not a spirituality. This is not to deny the experience of being comforted by God, but to warn against attempts to hide from life.

Passive Acceptance

In our culture, we are used to having professionals tell us about God. Most of us were taught beliefs about God and religion by our parents and by the religious institution our parents belonged to. We were probably trained to accept that others are more knowledgeable about a Higher Power and that we should accept their teachings. Perhaps we were encouraged to develop an inner faith, but one defined by a church, synagogue, or temple.

Maybe we were taught with the emphasis on the *otherness* of God. We learned to believe in a God who is a separate being outside ourselves, even in heaven, rather than an inner voice who speaks in our mind and heart. Perhaps an authority with religious credentials told us about God and the proper way to practice our faith. Often laypeople are denied access to positions of authority and responsibility within our religious community. Our attitude toward religion may have become one of passive acceptance, passive resistance, or rejection.

Ask yourself how many hours you spent in worship services, bored and simply waiting for the end. Many churches support passive worship by members of the congregation, who are trapped in pews. The service is "done" by ordained clergy, rabbis, or other officials, and the congregation attends.

In a church I have attended, the service begins with the invitation, "Let us stand and greet our celebrant by singing hymn number . . ." If there is one celebrant, what are the rest of us doing? In this situation, God can become a burden rather than a support, one more authority figure to please. People sometimes respond by either conforming and shutting down spiritually or rebelling and leaving their church.

Old Concepts of Our Higher Power

Unfortunately, much that is actually domination has also been presented in the name of a loving God. Often people in Twelve Step programs speak of their Higher Power "testing" them. But it is difficult to conceive of a God who loves us completely and also finds it necessary to test us. This kind of thinking comes from a concept of God as an authority figure we need to please. If someone loves us, he or she will not "test" us. We would be likely to feel controlled or judged more than loved.

Fear of God is often a part of shame-based spirituality. Many of us were taught to *fear* God, to see God as a big Eye in the Sky, always seeing what we are doing or even thinking. We have been taught that God, who is Love, also keeps a list of our faults and judges us. We are told that we can rely on God but also that we will be punished for our faults. We appear to lack humility if we protest. This is a double bind: contradictory statements on which we can't comment in a situation we can't escape. This can be crazy-making, but it is commonly taught in some religious institutions. Once we have accepted the concept of a punitive God, it is difficult for us to change our basic distrust.

If, as children, we were rarely given the freedom to make our own choices, we will have difficulty imagining such freedom. We will have no practice in accepting responsibility, and we may fear making mistakes. In this way, we don't trust our own inner wisdom, the guidance of our higher self.

Pleasing ourselves or others. Although the words of the Golden Rule read, *Love your neighbor as yourself,* most of us learned that God would be pleased if we loved our neighbors more. Self-sacrifice has been heavily promoted as a religious ideal. Unfortunately, this ideal nurtures us in assuming responsibility for others' feelings and behaviors and putting others' needs and wants before our own. This is generally understood as unhealthy codependency. In fact, a codependent relationship is usually based on being essential to the other person.

There is a difference between *codependent giving* and *true generosity.* It is not always easy to distinguish, but we can usually tell the difference by the feelings we have about our actions. True generosity feels good. It in itself is what we want; we are not looking for any results from our behavior.

Is there only one right belief? If we look at the world, we see that we are surrounded by diversity. In a rigid spirituality, differences are not always appreciated. Something different is harder to understand and can seem threatening. We may fear what we don't understand because we don't know how to control the unfamiliar. In an attempt to ward off the danger, we may develop "them and us," "right and wrong" belief systems. Only one church or faith community has the right answer, and guess whose that is! Some of us carry the idea of only one "right" belief system with us into our Twelve Step program.

Spiritual recovery and change. Recovering from shame-based spirituality isn't simply a matter of deciding to do things differently. Like other healing, it requires time, patience, and support for us to learn which of our spiritual patterns are restricting us and to become ready to let them transform. That's the difficult news. The good news is that the rewards of this recovery provide a new creative spiritual base that will allow continued transformation of ourselves and our lives.

Let's now move ahead by looking at how we can heal and grow in some areas important to our spirituality: the ability to surrender to a power of love greater than ourselves and the capability of loving ourselves and living from our own center.

Growing in Spirituality

A healthy spirituality

- encourages spiritual growth and models an image of a Higher Power that is not limiting.
- creates a container for experiencing God's unconditional love.
- provides the freedom to experience and express woundedness in all relationships, including ones we have with God and the church, for the purpose of healing.
- invites appropriate surrender and vulnerability.
- encourages commitment to spiritual values in one's life.

Developing an image of God. Although we can never develop an image that will fully reflect a Higher Power, some images are more helpful than others. In a spirituality that is growing and changing, our image of God changes also. Each picture we have allows us to experience a particular dimension of our Higher Power. Opening ourselves to new images of God means that God will be a varied and more visible presence in our life.

To more fully develop our ways of seeing God, we can look at how we now perceive our Higher Power and think about how that may impact us. When we can free ourselves to allow images of God to emerge, we will see different aspects when we need them. Sometimes that can be an image that we were taught in childhood, such as that of Jesus. We may find within us an old person who is a guide. The image could even be one we were taught was not God, such as a sensual woman. For quite a while, I had a non-image—God as a presence without any form. It is important to have an image of God that accepts the reality of who we are now, allows us to grow, and is truly larger than ourselves.

If you wish to look at this more deeply, you can spend time reviewing how you have seen God. To do this, write a description of all the pictures, experiences, or beliefs you have had of God or your Higher Power from childhood to the present time. How have they influenced your life? Your spirituality? What feelings does each image evoke?

You may wish to extend this exercise by doing it in a group and sharing your answers. Or you can use these impressions for meditation. Let yourself move back in age to your earliest memory of God. Let yourself feel whatever comes; let the image shift and change if it wishes. Remain with it as long as it feels right and then move to the next image that comes. Continue to do this until you have a sense of completion. When you have finished, write whatever you wish about your experience. This writing is important, since it brings your experience into focus and allows you to give voice to it.

Think about who your Higher Power would be if no one had ever told you about God. Write a want ad for the God you wish you had. You can connect with this image through meditation.

Getting closer to our Higher Power. Having developed an image of a Higher Power, we need to enhance that relationship, bringing our Higher Power into greater focus in our life. Centuries of spiritual traditions and volumes of books have addressed the question: How do we get closer to God? As is true in any relationship, part of the answer lies in spending time with God. This can mean starting a prayer or meditation practice or simply becoming more conscious of the presence of our Higher Power in our daily life. A friend spoke to me recently about the difference it made to her if she imagined God sitting next to her during the course of her day.

For some people, spiritually focused reading is helpful. For others, attending worship services, retreats, spiritual workshops, or meditation groups brings a feeling of closeness. If there is a spiritual tradition that appeals to you, you might get some suggestions from people in the community who practice it. Coming to know your Higher Power can also happen from listening to others talk about their spirituality, either at Twelve Step meetings or in private conversations. I have learned a lot from the practical, everyday spirituality of people in my life.

A meditation practice I find helpful is to find a quiet place, let myself relax by taking several deep breaths, and focus on becoming aware of the presence of my Higher Power. I realized one day that I didn't have to do ''something'' to make God appear. I simply needed to become conscious of a presence already there. When, inevitably, my mind wandered off, I simply returned to my original focus.

Clearing our decks of old baggage. Our wounds need healing to allow a new relationship with our Higher Power to grow, just as in a relationship with another person. One way Twelve Step programs suggest to deal with wounds and resentments is to do Fourth and Fifth Steps focused on God, church, or spirituality. Just as we need to clear our decks of past baggage with people, this may be needed with a higher power. As in any Fourth Step, we look closely at ourselves, our feelings, and our attitudes toward others. We don't do this to blame or determine right or wrong, but rather to release old hurts and resentments for our own well-being. Since our internal critic can have a field day with a Fourth Step, it is vital to do this Step with a sponsor, or we can end up feeling worse about ourselves.

Another way to deal with wounds is to bring them to our Higher Power for healing. We can do this in a meditative way by becoming quiet and allowing feelings to surface, remembering the grievance, and inviting our Higher Power to bring healing.

We can talk about our feelings and ask a friend or sponsor to be a listener. This person needs to understand that we aren't seeking advice or to be told that we are right. We simply need a friendly ear. In doing this, it is important to talk only about ourselves. Talking about how others have done us wrong will make things worse. It is our reaction to others' behavior that is important for healing. Sometimes, when I have talked things over with a friend, I experience it as my Higher Power talking to me through my friend. I have also been able to release unpleasant feelings by talking them to death with a series of people until there was no more "charge" left. By that time, even I was getting bored with my story.

The healing of old injuries, childhood wounds, and grief is often the focus of workshops or retreats. The presence of a group and a leader can be supportive, especially if wounds are deep. If it feels appropriate, talking with a carefully chosen spiritual advisor or psychotherapist can be beneficial.

Surrender to being loved by God. Surrender is not a popular idea. For some of us, it's what we do when we've lost the battle, or it means loss of control—the worst thing we can imagine. Or we can painfully remember surrendering ourselves to something or someone and then watching our life turn into disaster. When we surrender to something less than our Higher Power, we surrender to that which will seek to control us.

Psychology can help us to heal but cannot give us a place to surrender. When we surrender to God, we experience transformation, becoming increasingly like God. Maybe it isn't entirely correct to say that we surrender *to* God, rather we surrender to the experience of being *loved by* God.

An illusion fostered by some churches is that it is possible to "capture" God in a kind of permanent image of definition and dogma, that simply following rules and authority can lead us to God and assure us of a place in heaven. In reality, it is our openness to change and transformation and our freedom to expose our true selves that free us to feel union with God.

This is why Twelve Step programs work. They provide this freedom and enable us to discover a Higher Power on our own terms, our own understanding. We have a support community that sustains our connection with God. With this support, we can bear to face our denial, our woundedness, and our pain, and can come to a place of claiming our whole selves.

For a variety of reasons, some of us may choose to leave our original church. If we are conscious of our feelings and work through them, we will be able to retain the parts of our childhood spirituality that we treasure. Sometimes this can be the richness and wisdom of years of spirituality. Without healing, however, we may continue to believe there is a role that we must fit into, rather than a place where we can surrender. My personal goal is to find a framework, a process, a community for incorporating my own free expression of spirituality while retaining some of the resources of the tradition in which I was raised.

It is possible to live in assurance that we are lovable. This is what we strive for, what our dreams consist of. The love of God for "the least of these" is an old and valid message. In accepting ourselves as needing and relying on God, we have the strength to be vulnerable, to be loved fully, to be healed.

Making a commitment. In a healthy spirituality, there is a willingness to bring our spiritual values into our daily life. For instance, a commitment to the spiritual values of a Twelve Step program includes honesty, to the best of our ability, with ourselves and with others. This can be challenging and painful, as well as freeing. In a way, by practicing such honesty we allow a deeper source to touch and heal us, and we become willing to be vulnerable rather than defensive, capable of seeing truths about ourselves.

Talking about commitment and practicing what we believe can trigger old responses, either rebellion or reluctant conformity to a new list of *shoulds*. We may wish to adopt the values of a spiritual community, but it is important that the values also fit with our own personal values. To avoid slipping back into an old groove, it helps to explore feelings of resentment or resistance.

Others can be a helpful resource. If we like someone's spirituality, we can ask him or her about it. How does it work? Did the person have to overcome any of the problems we are now facing? We can talk about our struggles at our Twelve Step meetings.

Part of our commitment to spiritual values can be a desire to have our Higher Power guide our life. The Third Step is about making a decision to turn our will and our life over to the care of God. But how do we know what God's will is?

When the issue is sufficiently important, you can do a two-week *clarification* (to make clear) process. If you need to choose between path A or B, spend one week pretending you have made choice A, and one week living with choice B. Make it as real as possible. Write down your reactions or feelings as you live out your choice. During the week, spend time with your Higher Power and talk over your feelings and thoughts. Write about these conversations, also. After the two weeks, look over and pray about what you have written. You may wish to share it with a sponsor or friend and ask what he or she hears you saying. This can help to clarify what you truly desire, where God is leading you.

Loving Ourselves

We need to develop a spirituality that

- recognizes our uniqueness.
- challenges us to grow.
- encourages the healthy release of emotions.
- affirms us and discourages internal critics and perfectionism.
- helps to free our creative expression.

We must accept ourselves as we are before we are able to change. We also need to feel accepted by our Higher Power, affirmed as persons born as an irreplaceable part of the universe. For example, if I know there will never be another person just like me, with the same capacities and desires, abilities and faults, I have a hope of believing that I was born for a purpose that I can discover within myself. If the person I am has been treasured and nurtured, I can express my real self in the world. My spirituality can deepen that caring and give me a knowledge of my value before God.

A way to begin to do this is to think back over your life. Remember the moments when you felt very good about yourself and write them down. What were you doing? How were you perceived by others? Also, make a list of what you love to do, what feels good on a deep level and leaves you feeling good about yourself. The *desire* to do the good things we love comes from our Higher Power.

Keep these lists handy, as a reminder of what you want to do more of in your life. Have a goal that you will gradually increase the time you spend doing these things. This may be surprisingly difficult if it's new behavior, so remember to get help from a sponsor or therapist if you need it.

How you think your Higher Power would view your new behavior is important. If you imagine yourself to be in the presence of your Higher Power, is it all right to be free, fully yourself in your imperfection? Are you completely accepted, even loved? Does your Higher Power rejoice in your enjoyment of life? What are you feeling as you read these questions?

We talk of humility in the Twelve Step program. I define *humility* as having an accurate sense of ourselves. This means we are neither falsely modest nor grandiose about our abilities. Humility feels comfortable.

When we come to see our own value, we will begin to sense our authority and responsibility to do what is our unique task in the world. When we are involved in "doing our life," we will not feel victimized when things go wrong. As we begin to believe in ourselves, we'll stop asking the question, *What's wrong with me?* and start working on the questions, *What is happening here?* and *What action, if any, do I need to take?*

Continuing to Grow

A healthy spirituality challenges us to grow and to act from the power in being powerless. This *power* is an inner authority we feel when we act according to our genuine selves. We are powerless to manipulate our life or the lives of others. For a lot of my life, I saw the world as dangerous and I thought I needed to keep a tight grip on whatever happened to me. Out of fear, I tried my best to control whoever and whatever was around me. Gradually, through recovery, I have come to see the universe as friendly, and at its deepest, as awe-inspiring. With this new viewpoint, I can say yes to mystery and be willing to feel a little out of control, guided by a deeper part of myself.

We may have learned to fear change, associating it with loss, pain, and vulnerability. To begin to move away from that fear, we can try making a list of the changes in our life, ones that have happened and ones we are working toward. We may find that it is not the actual change we avoid, but the out-of-control feelings we have when changes come. With help, we can gradually walk through that fear.

We can become aware of how others increase our fear or discourage us from taking risks. When we learn to spot this, we can protect ourselves from taking on another's negativity. A sponsor in the program who has the kind of spirituality we want, people who will listen to us, and meetings that stress a spiritual program are valuable in learning to sort this out. We need to be loved into stretching our limits of what we think we can do. We need others to model their spirituality for us, so that we may see possibilities we are blind to by ourselves. When we see others model a way of living that inspires us, we can grow. As is said in the program, we want what they have.

Another part of growth is recognition of our needs. Along with the rules of *don't talk, don't trust, don't feel* that exist in addictive family and cultural systems, there is the rule *don't need*. As a result, we feel shame when we feel needy, and we try to maintain an independent posture. We confuse interdependence (we need other people) with dependence (I can't make it without you). This blocks our relationships with others and our Higher Power. We can find healing when we believe we are in a relationship of mutual desire for one another.

Getting in Touch with Our Feelings

In a healthy spirituality, all emotions are accepted, even welcomed. Strong emotions such as anger, despair, ecstasy, passion, and sexuality are used for personal and spiritual growth. Whatever childhood restrictions exist against experiencing certain feelings can be acknowledged.

Are there feelings that wouldn't meet your Higher Power's approval? Is anger okay? What about rage? Is it all right to be very needy with your Higher Power? What about resistance or rebellion? Or are you always supposed to be working a great program? How about sexual feelings, especially when they are evoked in what might be considered an inappropriate situation? It is important to distinguish, of course, between feelings and the actions we might take in response to them.

An exercise for working with these feelings is to remember times when you experienced a feeling that seemed unacceptable to you. Take one instance that you feel least uncomfortable about. Let yourself return to that time and place, making it as real as possible, remembering all that happened to evoke these feelings. Then bring your new image of a Higher Power into the scene with you. This Higher Power wants your healing.

Let your Higher Power speak to you about yourself and your feelings. Let this acceptance wash over you. If a critical voice enters, know that it is not your Higher Power's voice and ask it to leave. If it is insistent, tell it you will speak with it later, but you must have this time now. Invite your Higher Power to speak. You may also wish to talk with other persons involved in the incident in the presence of your Higher Power. When you feel finished, conclude the conversation in whatever way feels right. To deepen the experience, you may wish to write about it in a journal. You can repeat this exercise, gradually dealing with more difficult situations.

It is often easier to deal with these issues with the help of others. As with anything we feel shame about, it helps to talk about it, to reveal what is hidden. For example, it may be God we are angry at. Remembering a time when I was furious at God now makes me smile. I can feel good about it because I was able, with the support of a friend, to fully express my anger. Even knowing it wasn't reasonable, I could let my anger come out just because it was there. It felt wonderful!

Quieting Our Internal Critic

Another characteristic of a healthy spirituality is that it affirms us and discourages our destructive internal critics. In a healthy spirituality, we see ourselves as basically good. We know we are loved, not just out of the graciousness or sacrifice of an overly generous God, but because we are lovable. I can remember being told I ought to be grateful to God for loving me. I didn't agree, but I did develop a voice inside that said I was undeserving and ungrateful. This left me feeling manipulated, guilty, and wanting to avoid God. I now believe that my Higher Power's love for me is a freely given gift, as is my response. Without that freedom, my own response is only a pretense of love.

One of our internal critics may say that we must be perfect. Dealing with internal critics requires learning to distinguish the voices in our head from each other. When is it our crushing critic and when is it the voice of conscience from our Higher Power? One test is to see whether there are harsh and abusive judgments being made that create feelings of anxiety and despair. That's the critic! If we feel sadness along with the guilt and a desire to right the wrong, that is healthy regret. We need to distinguish between feeling bad about our actions and feeling bad about ourselves. Because making the distinction is initially confusing, it may help to talk it over with a sponsor or friend.

Creativity Brings Freedom

When we are living as our unique selves, we find we have a rich creativity available to us. We know how people are when they fall in love. They are a little silly, do unexpected things, and are freer than we are used to seeing them. Creativity is like that. We love into existence that which we wish to create. I believe that what we create also contains the love that brought us into existence.

I have never thought of the desire to create as love. I just knew I wanted to do it. By following my longing—

for a poem or a garden or rearranging the furniture—I do my part, and then that "spirit" dwells in me, bringing me joy and bringing forth a new birth. The discipline of gardening or writing or changing the living room is like a spiritual practice. Such disciplines include making choices, acquiring knowledge, and having a willingness to surrender to the art or to the urge to change the living room, so that which is deepest within us can be brought forth. I find that being creative makes me feel terribly vulnerable, challenged, and wholly satisfied.

The creative process is the opposite of the addictive process. The addictive spiral is repetitive, closing in on itself. It is boring and lifeless, with an illusion of security. Creativity is an explosion, moving in many directions at once, with an unpredictable destination. We need a sense of adventure, and a willingness and support system to deal with the fear and anxiety of feeling out of control.

People who are being transformed in recovery will unexpectedly share that they have decided to study the flute or take scuba lessons. This is a strong sign of new freedom to me, reflecting the importance of loving ourselves and being loved. If we are, it flows out to others without effort or resentment.

Someone once told me of a culture in which there was only one word that meant spirituality, creativity, and intuition. They were seen as basically the same thing. I think that concept is significant for our recovery from addiction. Creativity is life-giving, as our response to the arts tells us. Our spiritual beliefs need to support our own creativity in order to support our recovery.

Intimate Relationships with Others— Making the Connection

When I heard the idea stated that the patterns we have in relating to God are the same ones we have with people, I felt shocked, especially since I felt very distant from God at the time. Was I distant from my family and friends? I have come to see that I was. I questioned their capacity to be there for me, to fully accept me as I was. I revealed only part of myself and placed all the responsibility to be *acceptable,* even to define what that could mean, on myself. As I have been willing to be more open and less in control, an abundance of resources has opened for me from other people. And, not so amazingly, I have a new and creative connection with a power beyond myself.

This has become a guiding principle for me in my work with clients and my own inner work. Now I look to my relationships with people to understand better my relationship with my Higher Power. I look to my attitudes about God to learn more about the way I am with people and with myself.

It follows, then, that the dysfunctional relationship patterns we have with other people, we also have with God. Our problems with intimacy, control, boundaries, and even sexuality appear in our relationship with our Higher Power as well as in the areas where we can exercise freedom.

We're All in This Together

A spiritual community is an effective support for our relationship with a Higher Power. For many, Twelve Step programs fill this need. Others want to belong to different groups. My spiritual community brings a great richness to my life. I searched a long time for this community, looking for specific qualities. It was important to me that I feel accepted for who I am and that my gifts be welcomed. I also wanted to feel free to say yes or no to any commitment. I looked for caring people who worshipped and played together. I wanted to meet with people who were on a similar spiritual path to mine, who could be teachers as well as companions.

Especially important to me was the structure of this community. I wanted it to focus on bringing forth the gifts of the members. I wanted members to have both authority and responsibility. And I needed to feel good about myself when with them. I am grateful that my search has been so rewarded. I think such communities are difficult to find. But there is a great compensation in such support and acceptance: We begin to discover we have unexpected talents. We may even surprise ourselves with who we are!

Interpreting the Twelve Steps

For those in Twelve Step programs, the Steps themselves can sometimes lead to confusion. We may react with a variety of feelings to aspects of the Steps, such as turning our life over to God, asking God to remove our shortcomings, practicing prayer and meditation, and

doing God's will as best we can. It is important to realize that the spirituality outlined in the Twelve Steps is
mature, challenging, and profound. Some of what is
suggested has been done in monasteries and spiritual
communities for centuries. The Twelve Steps may be
"back-to-the-wall spirituality," but this spirituality is
high caliber, creates profound change, and provides un-
ceasing growth. If any part of the Steps seems wrong
or impossible to you, it's important to talk to a variety
of people about that part, especially those who have
many years in the program. People interpret the Steps
in different ways, and some of these ways may seem
more helpful to you than others. If they are understood
properly, the Steps may be challenging, but they will
help.

Seeing Today's Truth

Being in touch with our buried feelings about a
Higher Power can be difficult and threatening. Sometimes we feel we're "being bad" to criticize our religious teachings. Or we may be only too aware of our
resentments and wounds, yet reluctant to look more
closely at them. In reading the earlier parts of this chapter, did any of the descriptions seem familiar? Do they
describe aspects of your current spirituality? You can
use these as a checklist of problem areas.

Recognizing that a problem exists, coming out of denial, can be of great help in itself. Take time to step
back for some objectivity and distance as you would
with any relationship about which you had questions.
Write a letter to your Higher Power about how you're

feeling about your relationship with your Higher Power. Get as clear as you can about your present relationship. Is there anything you feel or think about your Higher Power that you believe is not okay? Remembering that any relationship can have both its wonderful parts and difficult areas, how would you describe your relationship? What's great and what's not? This will give you a clearer idea of where you are now.

All these aspects of spiritual freedom can be overwhelming. But recovery is doing one thing at a time. A question I have found helpful is, *What one thing am I willing to do now?* I can usually find something, and that's where I start. I let go of what comes next until later. You can choose what triggers a lot of feelings for you, or what feels least threatening. What matters is to begin, and you have already done that.

Healing is not a simple or an overnight process. It is a life's work, as we grow in our ability to allow love into our injured hearts. We are gradually and gently inviting in that which is other, yet is also ourselves, and making that precious presence welcome.

I would like to conclude with a poem I wrote that speaks to what this is all about.

You love me.
My faults diminish in my eyes.
For I do not see their reflection
In yours.

Healing Shame in Personal Relationships

Ronald Potter-Efron
Patricia Potter-Efron

The authors are therapists and have published books and journal articles on topics ranging from chemical dependency and family issues to shame and guilt.

Shame is corrosive. It eats away at dignity, pride, and self-respect. Unfortunately, many of us become embroiled in shame-based relationships that feature daily episodes of humiliation. Shaming relationships are dehumanizing. Each of us deserves to be treated with respect, no matter what the nature of our association with another person. Others equally deserve our respect. Any relationship that centers around shame dishonors its participants.

These relationships may be one-sided—only one member shames the other. One-way shame often occurs when one person enjoys a power advantage over the other. Two-way shaming relationships happen when both parties vigorously and regularly shame the other. These persons engage in shaming contests in which the object for each is to degrade the other more.

Few of us are strong enough to hold up to continuing shame attacks by people important to us. How can I feel really good when I am told over and over again that I am ugly, incompetent, worthless, or stupid? How can I feel healthy pride while listening to messages that I will never be good enough to satisfy my family, friends, or employer? The formula is simple: the more people are shamed by others, the more shameful they feel.

People who grew up with shame often believe that all relationships must be shame-centered. They expect to be told repeatedly that there is something wrong with them, or perhaps they feel they must do that to someone else. They have difficulty imagining that relationships can include mutual respect, dignity, and pride. The more a person has suffered shame, the more he expects it.

You may have strong feelings when reading this, especially if you are currently involved in a shaming relationship. It may be useful to keep a few thoughts in mind. First, someone who shames you may be unaware of it (not all shame episodes are deliberate). Second, you may be both a victim and a victimizer—this means that persons who are shamed by others often repeatedly shame other people as well. Try to notice how you are both the victim and attacker in the area of shame. Third, shame-based relationships can be changed. If both people in a relationship realize what is going on, they may be able to change.

Sometimes, people have become so involved in a shaming relationship, they are at a loss to break the cycle of shame. In such cases, a professional counselor may be able to help. Likewise, when people repeatedly find themselves in shaming relationships on all fronts, counseling is recommended. Shaming relationships can become respectful relationships when everyone involved understands the problem and commits to do something about it.

The issue is power. She uses her ability to shame others like a club. Colleagues at work, friends, family, all fear her sudden attacks. Just by looking at a person, she can make anyone feel small and puny. Shame is her best weapon—the way she keeps others under control.

"I had to get out of that marriage. My husband criticized everything I said or did. Now I'm in a relationship with a man who actually listens to what I say without interrupting or sneering at me. I can feel my pride returning."

"Sometimes I wonder if anybody in the whole world cares about me. Yes, I have a lot of people in my life. But they always want me to take care of them. When I have something I need help with or when I need to talk about my feelings, these people all seem to vanish. I feel more like a servant than a friend."

It only happens when she returns home for visits and holidays. She starts to feel small by the time she

opens the door. Then she gets weak and sick to her
stomach. She may be thirty-five years old, but she
cannot stop those old feelings of shame from coming
back. "Oh, there you are," says her mother. "Looks
like you've put on a few more pounds, dear."

We believe every person is entitled to a life free from
this kind of shame. Relationships can and must be built
around respect for this to happen. Let's look at the characteristics of shaming relationships.

The Shame-Based Relationship

A shame-based relationship is one where the people
shame each other routinely. Shame is so built into the
relationship that it seems normal. A day would feel unusual if shame were left out.

What does this kind of relationship look like? There
are actually two kinds. One is a *one-way shaming re-*
lationship in which most of the shaming is done by the
more powerful person to a less powerful one. The other
is a *two-way shaming relationship* where both persons
actively shame each other. Shamers are overly critical
of the person they are shaming. They watch for and are
quick to point out mistakes, using each blunder (real or
imagined) to validate their superiority.

Most of our examples refer to persons in intimate
relationships. Nevertheless, shaming can be a significant issue in many kinds of relationships. One-way
shaming relationships are most common when one individual has power over another. Typical examples are
employer/employee, parent/child, older sibling/younger

sibling (even as adult children), teacher/student, experienced member of an organization/newcomer, and some friendships in which one person is clearly in control.

Two-way shaming occurs most frequently in relationships between equally powerful persons, such as colleagues at work, stormy friendships, and mutually antagonistic siblings.

In an intimate or significant relationship, shamers know where others are most easily hurt and use that information to attack when there is conflict. They specialize in contempt and disdain for the very persons they supposedly love. They attack the independence of their partners by casting doubt on the partner's intelligence, common sense, and sanity. They actively seek to lower the other person by emphasizing shortcomings. In short, shamers diminish the people around them so they can feel better about themselves.

A relationship needs two persons, and shame-based relationships always feature at least one individual in the role of shame receiver. These shame receivers may accept criticism and shaming passively, without argument. Or they may fight it ferociously, even shaming the other person back in all-out warfare. Either way, they often remain stuck, unable to leave a bad relationship or to redesign the partnership around pride, dignity, and mutual appreciation. Shame-based relationships work with an unwritten rule that shaming is a necessary part of communication.

The Healthy Relationship

On the other hand, healthy relationships are built on mutual respect. Each person appreciates the other. Actually, the word *appreciation* is too weak; it is more appropriate to say that each person *honors* the other. Each recognizes the inner dignity of the other. They pay attention to the goodness they see and help bring out that goodness. Persons who find themselves in positive relationships will generally feel proud of themselves and of the other person.

How do you know if you are in a shame-based relationship? A clear signal is that you feel generally competent and worthwhile, except in the presence of a certain person. For example, a secretary who types for several bosses might feel fine with all but one of them. The secretary dreads seeing that boss because he only criticizes and demands the impossible. The secretary can never do good enough work to satisfy him—a sure trigger for shame.

Notice our emphasis on repetition. Most people shame another occasionally. The real problem occurs when shame is inherent in a relationship. Shame-based relationships are those in which a habit of shaming has developed and continues.

The Symptoms of Shame

If we get shamed regularly by another, we will probably develop many symptoms of shame. Some symptoms are that:

- we have trouble looking at the shamer;
- we feel very small, weak, exposed, and vulnerable in this person's presence;
- the longer we stay in the relationship, the worse we feel about ourselves; and
- we feel we are too damaged and unlovable to deserve any respect. Self-shaming thoughts add to our shame until we feel worthless and less than human.

People in shaming relationships often feel like children, as well as small and weak. This may be because they experienced many of the same shameful feelings as children: "My husband does the same things to me that my parents did—he even calls me the same mean names." Messages such as "You are unlovable" or "You don't belong," threats of abandonment and rejection, keeping secrets, physical and sexual abuse, perfectionism, and an over-concern with what others think, all help to transform a healthy relationship between two dignified adults into a shame-based relationship that reduces at least one member to the status of a child.

Unfortunately, once we live in one shaming relationship, it becomes easier to get into others just like it. This means that if we grew up in a shame-based family, we may be "attracted" late in life to persons who repeat the shaming maneuvers of our family. It also means that even people lucky enough to avoid shame as children can become shame-based adults if they find themselves in long-term shaming relationships. At first, these people may only feel shame in the presence of one specific person. But once people start to feel ashamed of themselves they begin to lose the ability to command respect from others. Many individuals finally discover that nearly every one of their significant relationships is centered around their shame. It's no wonder they feel hopeless.

Power through Shaming

Relationships often develop in which one member uses the ability to shame the other to increase or maintain control. For example, a man who repeatedly tells his wife that she is so bad in bed that no man could enjoy her, diminishes her belief in her attractiveness. Once she starts to believe him, she is less likely to consider leaving or even standing up to him as an equal. The more this man shames his wife, the more power he gains in the relationship.

Shaming may or may not be done purposely. Certainly not all such messages are deliberately designed to undermine the confidence of another person. Nevertheless, the effect of getting shamed regularly is that the shamed person will feel less and less powerful. One-way shaming relationships help keep one member in control of the other.

Shame may travel down the family power chain just like violence. The strongest member of the family shames the next most powerful. That person then shames the next and so on. Dad shames Mom who shames the oldest child, and so forth.

Power and the ability to shame another may go together. The more power people have, the more likely they are to get away with shame attacks on others. What can people say or do when their boss tells them that they are ignoramuses? Unfortunately, some employers believe they have a right to humiliate employees. And shamed people seldom feel strong enough to challenge those in power since they have lost their sense of inner worthiness.

Shame increases power differences over time. Two people who started out nearly equal will not stay that way if one is allowed to control the shame process. The shamer will gradually gain control of the relationship.

Some shamers use public humiliation to cement their power. Here, the shamer calls attention to another's deficits in front of other people. A woman who stresses her husband's clumsiness or his small paycheck may do so partly out of thoughtlessness or frustration. Frequent public attacks signify more than this—they make it seem like the person doing the shaming is superior. Here, this woman tells her audience that she is better than her husband since she has the right to complain about his deficiencies. She gains power and control unless her husband can directly challenge her accusations.

One-way shaming relationships distort human connections and are very damaging to the shame recipient. Shamers tend to be hurt less because they control the relationship. But they lose in being shamers. They lose deep intimacy with others while remaining aloof and superior. They lose the beauty of relationships based on mutual respect and dignity. The shamers pay a price for power.

The Mutually Shaming Relationship

Shame does not always travel in one direction only; it is often two-way. In these relationships, each person attacks the other whenever the opportunity arises. Contests even develop where the goal is to see which person can best embarrass or degrade the other. Shame is used as a weapon.

Witnesses to these shame battles may feel horrified as they watch the pair try to destroy each other. The longer the fight goes on, the meaner it gets. The partners in this battle may finally forget about tact and discretion. Instead, in public they air things which ought to be private about the other person. One may score a victory over the other, but trust is also destroyed.

Both participants in mutually shaming relationships get badly damaged. Their worst features are exposed as their personalities come under constant attack. Any dignity they had is drowned in an ocean of mutual recriminations.

Sometimes, shaming couples get locked into rigid roles that only increase their shame. One example is "The Drunk and the Bitcher" game in which the more the drunk drinks, the more the bitcher bitches, and the more the bitcher bitches, the more the drunk drinks. Each can eventually despise the other. Each may believe the other is the shamer and he or she is an innocent victim. Neither can think of any way to break out of these terribly destructive roles.

The theme of mutually shaming relationships is contempt. The longer people are in the relationship, the less they respect their partners. They may also begin to despise themselves for participating in the daily shame battles. "How can I sink so low? I hate hearing myself calling him those names, and I know I'm hurting him just like he hurts me when he attacks." If only the shamers could stop striking out. Unfortunately, she may not quit shaming him because she thinks she needs to defend herself against his shame attacks. The victim of a shame assault may attack the person who shamed him as a defense. Shame begets shame.

Shame can lock two persons into constant conflict. Neither one of them ends the relationship because that would be the final defeat. Their shame battles end in exhaustion, not victory for either side. Truces become harder and harder to arrange because both people feel too vulnerable when they put down their shame weapons. These people might have no relationship at all if they were not shaming each other. Shame becomes the cement that binds them together.

Healing Shame in Current Relationships

They are an amazing couple. He tells her she is a lousy mother while she faults his inability to show feelings. They go on and on like that. Then they feel awful about what has happened to them—how hate and shame have replaced love and honor. They need to call a truce, but each is afraid to stop attacking the other.

"For years I took his inventory. I watched his every movement for signs that he wanted to put me down. I never even noticed how I shamed him. If I did, I justified my behavior by telling myself I was only de-

fending myself. Things didn't start to change until I made some commitments to quit shaming him.''

"Enough is enough. I've explained to my partner that I will no longer tolerate his abuse. But he refused to change. Every day he still calls me names in front of our friends. He says I deserve it, and he won't accept any responsibility for his actions. I can't live with him much longer. How can I feel less shame when he deliberately adds to my shame?''

Almost everyone likes working for John, a manager in a large firm. His employees know he will treat them with respect and dignity even when he disagrees with their point of view. In return, they honor him. He is the one manager they never insult or ridicule.

To review, shame-based relationships are those that center around excessive shame. This shame may flow in one direction only (usually from a more powerful individual toward a weaker person), or it might get passed from one person to another through mutually destructive shame contests. Either way, relationships built around shame damage the participants, even those who seem to gain power and control. Shame-based relationships damage the dignity of everybody and minimize the possibility for deeper intimacy.

The goal, then, is to exchange or alter shame-based relationships to relationships that center around honor, respect, and dignity. Here are some guidelines designed to help you reach that goal:

1. Begin by becoming aware of how you shame others in your important relationships.
2. Notice what you gain through shaming others.
3. Notice what damage occurs to yourself and others through your shaming behavior.
4. Connect your shaming behaviors with your own shame and self-hatred issues.
5. Make a commitment to quit shaming others, regardless of their behavior toward you.
6. Replace shaming behavior with respectful actions toward others.
7. Notice how you are shamed by significant others and the damage done.
8. Confront and challenge shaming behavior that is directed toward you.
9. Consider leaving relationships that remain shame-based.
10. Make and keep a commitment to nurture nonshaming relationships.

Begin by Becoming Aware of How You Shame Others in Your Important Relationships

Frankly, it is much easier for most people to pay attention to how others shame them than to look at their own shaming actions. We suggest that it is more productive to begin by examining our tendency to shame the important persons in our lives. This is particularly true for two-way shaming relationships in which both parties use shame as a weapon to gain power and control.

Here is a typical example: A couple complains that

all they do is bicker and fight. Then each spends hours pointing out exactly what the other does that distresses him or her. Neither partner has much interest in listening to the other; they are too busy attacking. Each is well aware of how he or she is being shamed but both are unwilling to change their shaming behavior.

Nobody gives up power easily. That general principle leads to a more specific one: nobody gives up the power of shaming others easily. So, before asking someone to stop shaming you, it's vital that you honestly evaluate your own words, thoughts, and actions.

Start by recognizing your most direct and forceful shame attacks. These are the deliberate insults you heap on your partner (or other people important in your life). Some of these insults might be spoken in public—a good name for these is *humiliations*. Others may be done in private, but they are perhaps equally damaging. These insults are usually predictable in a long-term relationship. They are open signs of contempt for the other person. When they work, they diminish and weaken your partner.

Then think about the more subtle ways that you demean others. Do you roll your eyes in disgust when your children try to talk with you? Do you interrupt your partner regularly because you think you know so much more? Do you chuckle a little too often at his serious remarks? Are you so bored with someone's remarks that you don't even listen when she speaks? How else do you subtly shame the people around you?

What if you find no evidence that you shame another person? First, go back and look again. Remember that it is hard to face this part of ourselves, so it is easy to deny shaming behavior. Next, check with others directly, by asking them if and when they feel shamed by you, and by noticing their reactions to your behavior. Watch for times when the persons you speak with look embarrassed or appear to get smaller and weaker. Also remember that one defense against shame is rage. Someone who suddenly gets very angry with you may be responding with shame to something you said.

Perhaps you don't shame another who does shame you. Then you are the recipient of shame in a one-way relationship. Even so, be sure to read the next several steps in the guidelines as another way to check out the possibility that you are shaming others more than you know. Then focus your energy on the last few suggestions that concentrate on confronting shame from others.

Notice What You Gain Through Shaming Others

One of the reasons a person shames others is simply out of habit. Sometimes shame has become so common that it's used automatically. People may shame others for many additional reasons—a few reasons are the desire for power and control, a wish to feel superior, and as a way to defend against exposure of their own shame.

"I am stronger than you" is the sometimes hidden message of those who use shame to gain power and control over another person. He tells her that she is weak, ineffectual, useless, and feeble. He points to her shortcomings as evidence that he should take over control of her life. The message may be crude ("You're so irresponsible I have to manage our checkbook'') or subtle (''Keep trying, dear. One of these days maybe you will be able to handle money. Until then, though, I better write all our checks'').

''I am better than you'' is the message that comes from a shamer who wants to feel superior to her partner or associate. She focuses on the other's personal or cultural ''shortcomings.'' For instance, she might tell her partner that he is too crude, uneducated, or simplistic ever to be her equal. This person shames others so she can continue to feel specially gifted. She uses shame to maintain her prestige.

''Better you than me'' is usually the secret thought of a person who shames others so they can't shame him. This defensive maneuver is common in two-way shaming relationships in which shame contests occur often. The idea is to get in the first punch. For example, if a woman can attack her husband for his laziness before he can assail her eating habits, she protects against the exposure of her shame.

Shame can help keep a person feeling powerful, prestigious, and safe. Why, then, would a person voluntarily relinquish this excellent weapon? Indeed, some individuals refuse to quit shaming others. They prefer power over intimacy. They view treating others with respect and dignity as a sign of weakness.

We suggest that most people who quit shaming others do so for a selfish reason. They finally recognize that they can't heal their own shame by pretending they are somehow stronger, wiser, or better than everybody else. They find that they can only move toward the principles of humanity, humility, competence, and autonomy by giving up both their claims to inherent superiority and inferiority. They can't find their place in the human community until they allow the people they love to be human.

Individuals who want to develop nonshaming relationships with others must take a good look at what they have gained through shaming others. Then, with this knowledge, they can decide whether or not they want to change their behavior.

Notice What Damage Occurs to Yourself and Others Through Your Shaming Behavior

Shame attacks hurt the people we care about. Now is the time to pay careful attention to this damage. Do your children stumble to their rooms and refuse to come out, even to play, after you shame them? Does your partner look embarrassed when you hammer away at some topic better left alone? Do your work associates flinch at your savage attacks on their personalities?

It takes no great skill to harm another individual through shame. Anybody can do it. Most people are vulnerable to shame because they need approval from the important persons in their lives. We believe that it takes more skill to refrain from shaming others and, instead, to demonstrate consistent caring and appreciation.

Be specific here. Listen to the difference between these two statements:

"I guess I hurt her with my shame. I must have, but I don't know how."

"When I told her she was stupid I could see the pain in her face—the way she blinked her eyes and dropped her head."

Notice that the second comment provides exact cues for the shamer. From now on, he can remind himself that he doesn't want to say or do things that cause that response in another. And, if he does notice someone respond that way, he'll be able to tell himself that he may have tapped that person's shame. He can then choose to change his actions before more damage is done.

The shamer should also attend to what damage he does to himself. Does he feel worse instead of better after a shame attack? Does he feel isolated and alone? Does he invite others to shame him, starting a shame contest? Does he feel less than fully human when he shames others? Does he feel guilty? Here, too, he needs to be as specific as possible. Vague responses are not useful because they do not lead to real behavioral changes.

Warning: Do not rush to make everything right all at once. You may be overwhelmed with shame and guilt if you do. Take your time. Learn about yourself. Start slow and easy. Give yourself time to make real changes in your life.

Connect Your Shaming Behaviors with Your Own Shame and Self-Hatred Issues

Many habitual shamers are people who are themselves deeply ashamed and full of self-hatred. Furthermore, they often shame others with statements they really believe about themselves. For example, a worker who calls her co-worker boring and dull may secretly believe that she—herself—is boring and dull. This person "projects" her shame outside of herself—she gives it away so she won't feel defective.

It's important to consider this possibility when you study how you shame others. Pay attention in particular to statements that you use most frequently—those are the ones you most likely believe about yourself. Also, look for shaming statements that don't fit the other person at all, such as calling someone lazy who obviously is not. Here again, you may be tapping your own projected shame.

This doesn't mean every nasty comment you make is about your own shame, nor can you assume that all the shaming statements people direct at you are projections of their own shame. There are many reasons people shame each other.

Shaming another may hide our own shame from us, but it can't heal our shame. We must have the courage to face our shame, rather than trying to give it away by blaming and attacking another. The next step after awareness is to make a commitment to quit shaming others with our own self-hatred.

Make a Commitment to Quit Shaming Others, Regardless of Their Behavior Toward You

We believe that shaming another human being damages the inner dignity of the shamer. The individual who attacks others moves away from her own humanity, humility, autonomy, and competence. Shaming others, in the long run, increases a person's shame instead of lessening it. The person who wants to relieve her own shame needs to make a serious commitment to refrain from shaming others.

"I agree that I should stop shaming my spouse, but what if he keeps on shaming me? I will only agree to quit if he does." This individual gives responsibility for her own decisions to her husband. She allows him to decide how she will run her life. If he agrees to the truce and then reneges, she would have a perfect excuse to return to her own shaming activities.

The point is that we can't wait for the world to become a nicer place. We can't wait until everybody else quits shaming us before we make a serious commitment to change our behavior. Self-determination means we are responsible for our own behavior. The time to stop shaming the people we care about is as soon as we realize that belittling them only diminishes ourselves.

If you habitually tell someone she is fat and ugly, then today make a commitment to erase that phrase from your vocabulary. Don't allow yourself to nitpick somebody's tiny failings. Decide today that you will no longer publicly humiliate your partner. Then keep those commitments. Don't *try* not to shame others—*just don't shame them.* If you do break this promise, don't attack yourself. Instead, immediately correct the situation by apologizing to the person you shamed and renewing your promise not to shame others. Remember also to watch and manage your nonverbal behavior so that you don't shame another with a dirty look.

Sometimes, others will respond positively to your changes. They might stop shaming you when you are no longer degrading them. Try to consider those changes as wonderful bonuses but not as the payoff for your decision. The real reward for not shaming others is that you gain greater self-respect. People who refuse to shame others are less likely to shame themselves.

Replace Shaming Behavior with Respectful Actions Toward Others

People create communication vacuums when they stop one kind of behavior but don't replace it with another. For example, one couple agreed to quit shaming each other after realizing the damage they were doing to the relationship. But then they found they had nothing to talk about. Their partnership was so shame-based that it was virtually empty in the absence of continuous mutual criticism.

Praise, respect, and appreciation are positive ways to replace shaming words and actions. These new behaviors may be difficult at first for the habitual shamer. Many persons will have to make a conscious effort to learn how to speak in a nonshaming manner. First, they need to pay attention to the good things, instead of the flaws, about others. Second, they have to learn how to tell others that they respect and appreciate them. Last, they need to resist the urge to follow praise with condemnation, which returns them to shaming behavior.

Here are a few ideas to remember if you accept the goal of learning to speak in nonshaming ways:

1. Begin each day with a renewed commitment to respect the dignity of others.
2. Consciously notice the positive words and actions of the people you care for.
3. Look for the inner goodness of each person in your life. Respect is based on an appreciation of others as human beings, regardless of their specific behaviors.
4. Tell others that they are good, good enough, lovable, and important. Don't let the words get stuck in your throat.
5. Never use praise to prepare the ground for criticism ("I sure like the way you cooked dinner tonight, but. . .")
6. You can respect people and still disagree with them. Some conflict is inevitable in a relationship, but that is no excuse for shaming behaviors.
7. Don't expect or demand praise in return when you express your appreciation. You might not get it. Don't use that as a justification to attack.
8. Pay attention to the changes that occur inside you when you substitute respect for shame. Remember that you are the ultimate beneficiary of this new behavior. Respecting others will eventually increase your own self-respect.

Notice How You Are Shamed by Significant Others and the Damage Done

Once you have made a commitment to respect others, you are ready to pay serious attention to how others shame you. This does not mean you have to be perfect or that you will never shame another individual again. That is impossible. The point is, you can't realistically

expect another person to quit shaming you until you
have altered your own shaming behavior.

Begin with a current relationship in which you suspect that you are shamed frequently. Take a few days
or a week simply to study the shaming patterns that
occur. Don't forget to notice how you shame the other
individual as well as how that person shames you.

Watch carefully for repeated phrases and actions—
shaming habits that have developed, such as one person
condescendingly patting the other on the head or regularly ignoring what the other says. Notice both subtle
and crude attacks on your self-esteem. Watch for times
when someone seems to deliberately shame you, in
contrast to occasions when shaming seems to happen
less consciously. You may even notice times when you
feel ashamed by messages that may have actually been
intended to make you feel better. Try to remember that,
in many relationships, shame is more often dealt out
accidentally than with the desire to inflict permanent
damage.

A message or action is shaming, regardless of the
intent of the sender, when the recipient feels less human, less humble (in the sense of being no better or
worse than others), less autonomous, or less competent. It is important that you learn how another person's
shaming messages harm you. Asking yourself these
questions may help you get in touch with the harm done:

- Do I feel somehow dirty or unclean after conversations with a particular individual?
- Do I feel less intelligent or competent than I did before the discussion?

- Do I sense that this person can't accept me unless I give up my independence and do exactly what he or she wants?
- Do I feel small and childlike on a regular basis in the presence of this person?
- Does this person talk about my inadequacies and shortcomings quite often?

The above questions help identify the immediate effects of shame. But it is also necessary to attend to long-term consequences. Ask yourself a few more questions that focus on at least the last several months in your relationship with another individual.

- Overall, how has this person helped me feel that I am a worthwhile human being?
- How has this person diminished my sense of self-worth?
- Does this relationship nurture my inner strength or feed my weaknesses?
- What about this connection decreases or increases my shame?
- Is this relationship moving toward or away from mutual respect?
- Does my life seem more or less meaningful now than before, and how does that connect with this relationship?

Shame causes damage. Your task here is to become more aware of how you are being damaged by shame directed at you. Be specific, just as you were when you assessed how you damaged others with your own shaming behavior. Try not to minimize or exaggerate—just be as accurate as you can. You will soon need to speak clearly to the person who is shaming you, as you confront and challenge shaming behaviors.

Confront and Challenge Shaming Behavior Directed Toward You

Now we have reached the decision point. Do we proceed, with the knowledge we've gathered, to confront the people who shame us? Do we dare risk their denial, anger, defensiveness, and ability to shame us all the more, in order to gain respectful and appreciative treatment? Are we willing to face the fears of abandonment—fears that reflect our doubts about our own validity as human beings?

It's scary to challenge someone who has the power to shame us. However, the longer the shaming continues uncontested, the more damage is done to the receiver. Shame, unchallenged, works its way into the core of an individual's self-concept. Sooner or later, a person who wants healthy pride and dignity will have to confront those who shame her. She will need to tell those people that she is no longer willing to participate in relationships that add to her sense of shame. She will request specific changes in the words and actions of those individuals to promote respect, rather than shame.

Here are a few suggestions if you do decide to confront shaming behavior:

• Be firm and clear about your purpose—know exactly what you want from the other person.

- Be prepared to offer specific examples of behavior that triggered your shame.
- Model respectful behavior both toward yourself and others during the confrontation—above all, do not shame anyone.
- Don't back down in the face of another's immediate defensiveness, hurt, or threats.
- Remember that the goal is not to punish, but to alter the current and future behavior of the other person.
- Expect gradual change over a long period of time, rather than immediate success.
- Realize that you will probably need to have several conversations with the other person before you both understand the issue completely.
- Be prepared to deal with the topic of how you shame the person who shames you.

Perhaps all these ideas sound complicated. Actually, only one act stands out as a necessity. *Somehow, you must inform the persons who regularly shame you that you will no longer accept that behavior.* Shame makes a person sick. It is time to insist that the important persons in your life contribute to your health instead.

Consider Leaving Relationships That Remain Shame-Based

Shaming habits are hard to break, even when both individuals want to quit shaming each other. They are even more difficult to alter when one or both continue shaming the other. This means that the person who challenges a shame-based relationship may need to leave that relationship if the shaming continues unabated.

Shamed persons may dread the idea of leaving a partner (employer, friend) who shames them. They fear that no one else will ever want them. Sadly, they are paralyzed by the very shame they can't imagine escaping. They have lost faith that they deserve a good place in the world.

No other person should tell you when to leave a shaming relationship. Those decisions are too personal and vital for others to judge from afar. But it is reasonable to ask someone what he or she hopes to gain by staying in such a relationship. It may be time to get out if the answer to this question is more shame, blame, and unhappiness.

Some shame-based relationships can't be salvaged. Shame permeates and controls so many interactions that change is impossible. Furthermore, some people seem incapable of, or uninterested in, learning and practicing respectful communication. These relationships may eventually have to be ended in order to develop self-respect.

Make and Keep a Commitment to Nurture Nonshaming Relationships

Those who confront shaming behavior in their current relationships will discover that the shame episodes gradually diminish. First, they shame others less frequently. Second, they accept fewer shame attacks from others. Last, they will probably notice that they are more attracted to others who practice respect rather than shame.

Mutually nonshaming relationships must be nurtured. They consist of people who consciously choose to treat each other with dignity and respect. All parties need the courage to confront shaming behavior as it occurs so it can be changed before much damage is done. Above all, individuals in respectful relationships must remember that their partners, friends, and associates deserve to be treated with fairness.

Mutually respectful relationships help heal the wounds of shame. They are only possible when the participants make and regularly renew their vow to refrain from shaming each other. They are sustained through commitment, communications, and sometimes hard work.

"Stick with the winners" is a phrase often repeated in self-help communities such as Alcoholics Anonymous. We want to offer the same suggestion. Here the winners are those individuals who treat each other and themselves with honor, respect, and dignity. These are persons who choose not to shame each other.

Shame in current relationships can be healed. The process begins with checking out whether you shame others. You may then decide to convert your shaming into nonshaming behavior. The next major step is to confront and challenge others whose shaming attacks damage you.

People who are shamed regularly have difficulty feeling good about themselves. Therefore, a goal is to develop and maintain mutually respectful relationships. While these relationships may have been deeply shaming, we believe such relationships can be altered—provided both members want change or at least one of them refuses to continue living with shame. But some relationships are incapable of a pattern of mutual respect. In such cases, you may choose to leave the association in order to protect your self-worth.

Exercises

Exercise One

A shaming relationship is based on repeated and routine behaviors that send the message that something is wrong with a person. Using the following checklist, evaluate your relationship with a significant other person by underlining each statement which is true.

The person

1. says or implies that I am fat, ugly, stupid, bad, incompetent, inadequate, unlovable, or worthless.
2. calls me names.
3. swears at me.
4. ignores me as if what I say and do is not important.
5. criticizes my tastes and choices regularly.
6. criticizes quite often what I do and how I do it.
7. criticizes me or makes fun of me in front of others.
8. tells me I am not as good as other people.

9. tells me that how I feel is stupid, irrelevant, or unimportant.
10. tells me that he or she is superior to me.
11. hits, pushes, slaps, kicks, or otherwise physically abuses me.
12. often acts disappointed, angry, or disgusted with me.
13. tells me I am weird or crazy.
14. refuses to touch me or only touches me for sex or punishment.
15. tells me I should die, disappear, get rid of myself, or get lost.

Now look at your own behavior with this person. Shaming relationships are all too often relationships where both people are shamers, but each only looks at what the other person is doing wrong. So reverse the relationship and do the checklist below, again underlining each statement that applies. Be self-aware and honest as you do this.

1. I say or imply that this person is fat, ugly, stupid, bad, incompetent, inadequate, unlovable, or worthless.
2. I call the person names.
3. I swear at the person.
4. I ignore the person as if what he or she does and says is not important.
5. I criticize this person's tastes and choices regularly.
6. Quite often, I criticize what the person does and how he or she does it.
7. I make fun of this person in front of others.

8. I tell the person that he or she is not as good as other people.
9. I tell this person that how he or she feels is stupid, irrelevant, or unimportant.
10. I tell the person that I am superior to him or her.
11. I hit, push, slap, kick, or otherwise physically abuse this person.
12. I often act disappointed, angry, or disgusted with the person.
13. I tell this person that he or she is weird or crazy.
14. I refuse to touch the person or only do so for sex or punishment.
15. I tell this person that he or she should die, disappear, get rid of him- or herself, or get lost.

Exercise Two

On a sheet of paper, do the following tasks:

Judy and Ray have been married two years. Judy comes from a perfectionistic family where she learned that shame keeps people under control. Judy says Ray should help her by doing the dishes, but when he does do them, she shames him for not doing the glasses first, not rinsing the plates in a special way, and not scrubbing the pans "correctly." Each time he does the dishes, she seems to find something wrong in what he does. This same thing happens when he cleans the living room, does the wash, or drives the car.

How do you think Ray feels about himself? How does he feel about Judy? How does Judy feel about herself? How does she feel about Ray?

1. List any one-way shaming relationships in which you have been the person shamed.
2. List any one-way shaming relationships in which you have been the shamer.
3. List any two-way shaming relationships you have been involved in.
4. Do you see any pattern in these relationships? Write down what you notice.
5. Now list any nonshaming relationships you have been involved in.
6. How are the nonshaming relationships different?
7. List the main ways you shame others.

Exercise Three

Note any of the following items that you gain as a result of shaming others. List any others you think of.

Feel I'm in control	Stop inner criticism
Pleasure	Get to share misery
Don't have to do things	Get tension release
Get to be best	Get the last word
Stop their criticism	Get to be selfish
Get revenge	Know I'm superior
Physical power	Get extra help
Get to be right	Don't have to feel
Safe distance	Get to complain
Get to be angry	Get what I want
Feel powerful	

Notice the qualities on the following list you lose from

shaming others. Note those that others lose when you shame them.

Confidence	Love	Closeness
Pride	Peace of mind	Respect
Self-respect	Companionship	Trust
Spontaneity	Dignity	Playfulness

Specifically, how do you see that others are damaged when you shame them?

Exercise Four

Parents who are ashamed of their youthful "wildness" may shame their children by accusing them of sexual behavior without much justification. Children who have just violated a rule may shame their little brother or sister for being bad when they have done nothing. Partners "project" like this, too, shaming each other because they are seeing their own flaws. This week, make a list of everything you shame in others that are also flaws you see in yourself. Be honest!

Exercise Five

Make a commitment to stop specific shaming behaviors. Any violation of these commitments to yourself means an apology to the other person, no matter how he or she behaves. Your commitment is to dignity and self-respect based on your own behavior. Review your behavior toward that person, checking your results weekly.

Exercise Six

Now you are ready to consider how others shame you. Choose just one to start with—this could be a partner, parent, child, sibling, employer, colleague, or counselor. Write on a sheet of paper the shaming messages directed at you. Remember those messages that say you are not good, not good enough, not lovable, don't belong, and should not exist. These messages may be transmitted to you verbally or nonverbally.

Choose one shaming message to challenge first. As you see the results, you may wish to challenge other messages. Be clear, specific, and respectful in your challenges. Be sure to use the guidelines noted in the section on confronting and challenging shaming behavior directed toward you. Respond to this exercise on a separate sheet of paper.

1. Shaming message I get now:
2. Nonshaming message I want to get instead:
3. Two things I will say or do during this conversation:
4. Two things I will not say or do during this conversation:
5. If the person I confront gets defensive, I will:
6. If the person I confront apologizes, I will:
7. No matter what, I will:
8. No matter what, I will not:

Those who surround themselves with shaming people may believe they deserve to be treated negatively. For a happy, healthy life, we must surround ourselves with others with whom we share appreciation and dignity. Everybody deserves to be treated respectfully.

Self-Esteem: Why We Hide the Truth About Ourselves

Marie Lindquist

Marie Lindquist is the author of several wellness books for young adults. She lives in New York City.

Accepting Yourself

Ask any psychiatrist, counselor, or spiritual leader what one of the biggest human problems is and you'll get a unanimous answer: lack of self-esteem. This is tragic because all of us desperately want to accept ourselves and move through life with confidence. We want this so badly we go to great lengths to get it.

We believe that we get self-esteem by

- disowning parts of the self we feel are unacceptable;
- trying too hard to win the world's approval;
- creating masks of superiority;

- not acting spontaneously but instead acting in ways we hope will be acceptable to others;
- avoiding to set some goals for fear we will not achieve them;
- denying emotions because they conflict with an idealized view of ourselves.

The list could go on and on, with only one result: *None* of these ploys works. All of them go *against* the self. In some ways, they deny or disown an important part of our being.

Many people resist accepting themselves because they fear it means "giving up." A friend once asked me, "If I accept myself as I am, isn't that like raising the white flag? Isn't it like saying *'This is the best I can do'?*" No, it isn't.

The confusion begins when we are young, when our mother or father tells us we are "bad" (unacceptable) for spilling our milk, hiding grandpa's slippers, or pulling the dog's tail. What our parents mean, of course, is that our *behavior* is bad. Few parents have the time or the insight to make this clear to the child. Even if they do, the young mind may not distinguish the difference. Since we want our parents' love, it is likely that any show of disapproval will be interpreted as rejection.

Hence, we incorporate into our life script a strict idea of what "acceptable" is, of exactly what is required to win approval. As we grow up, influences outside the home further embellish and restrict that ideal. Schools, teachers, advertising, the media, and popular culture all contribute to the long list of "shoulds" we carry around inside us. At the moment, the contemporary American woman should be youthful, glamorous, slender, sexy, witty, and well-read; she should be career-oriented without slighting her role as mother, homemaker, and helpmate. Her male counterpart must be tough at work, sensitive at home, available to his children, supportive to his wife, and a dynamo in the bedroom. With unrealistic standards like these, it's no wonder that most of us walk around feeling anything but adequate.

Self-acceptance begins with banishing artificially imposed *shoulds* from your thinking. You don't have to become a doctor to be okay, just because being a doctor is one of the goals your parents set for you. You don't have to *have it all* if having it all is going to put you six feet under. Nor does self-acceptance mean that you have decided to remain exactly as you are today.

Self-acceptance means accepting yourself as a work-in-progress. It means believing that you are okay in spite of your flaws and believing that you have the strength and the power to change.

But where, you ask, is that belief to come from? How can a nonbeliever suddenly become a believer?

One way is to root out the negative messages embedded in the Parent part of your personality. Most of us can close our eyes and let all sorts of voices from the past surface.

"Why can't you be more like your brother?" (Don't be you—be a copy of someone else.)

"You don't have the sense God gave a goose." (You're dumb.)

"Don't touch yourself there." (You're dirty.)

"Can't you ever do anything right?" (You'll never change.)

These voices have become part of the negative Parent within us. We go on listening to them year in and year out, allowing them to bury our self-esteem. But we don't have to. We can replace them with affirmations—fresh and positive messages.

"You are lovable."

"You are kind and caring."

"You have what it takes to succeed."

All of these are examples of affirmations. When you make up your own affirmations, tailor them to counteract the negative messages in your life script.

The opinion we have of ourselves isn't just based on beliefs—it's also based on actions. We observe ourselves just as we observe others, and when the belief that we aren't good enough is coupled with actions of self-neglect and abuse, self-esteem sinks even further. The alcoholic who drinks to cover up feelings of inadequacy, for example, will feel even *more* inadequate as he sees himself losing control of his life.

There are certain things each of us must pursue in order to feel good about ourselves. These building blocks of self-esteem are

- *A sense of worthiness*. Individuals need to see themselves as *deserving* of attention and esteem. The person who sees himself as undeserving will, whether that assessment is true or not, act in self-neglectful and abusive ways.
- *A sense of effectiveness*. No one can feel good about herself if she feels impotent. The person who undermines her ability to act, who becomes a passive onlooker in life, will suffer a loss of self-esteem.

- *Self-regulation.* One of the hallmarks of maturity is the ability to override our impulses. The person who feels that some area of his life is out of control will not respect himself as he respects those who are in control.

- *Meaningful work.* Freud said there are just two things that count in life: work and love. While this is a bit narrow for most of us, work is certainly one of the necessary ingredients for a full life. Work does not always have to be creative, well-paid, or stimulating to be meaningful. A factory worker may dislike her job but find it meaningful because it allows her to care for her family and to maintain independence.

- *Pleasure for pleasure's sake.* Do you remember how good playing made you feel when you were a child? As adults we often lose the ability to play, but we never lose the need or the desire. *Pleasure for pleasure's sake* means playing in the true sense of the word, for the pure joy of it. It means playing golf for the pleasure of seeing the sun on the grass and the satisfaction of hearing the ball roll into the cup—not for the competitiveness of the game or the dividend of talking business at every opportunity.

- *To give strokes.* The exchange of friendly words is the exchange of affection. The person who can give strokes freely and spontaneously will appreciate himself as a caring person.

- *To receive strokes.* How others think of us will affect the way we feel about ourselves. The person who can remain open, who can receive and appreciate the strokes given to her by others, will have a higher degree of self-esteem than the person who feels isolated from others.

When thinking about self-acceptance, it's important to remember that *feelings follow actions*. What you do will influence the way you feel. If you take care of yourself and treat yourself *as if* you are worthy, you will begin to *feel* worthy. And this is true for the other components of self-esteem. If you are having a difficult time directing your thoughts, concentrate on directing your actions—your feelings will follow.

Assuming Risk

All of life's great achievements begin the same way: by taking a risk. The child who tries to walk risks falling on his bottom. The politician who runs for office risks the humiliation of losing by a landslide. The artist who creates something risks being scoffed at. And the person who discloses himself risks being misunderstood and rejected.

While it may be easy for us to risk in other areas of life, it is often extremely difficult to do so in the emotional realm.

How can we risk-proof ourselves in preparation for intimacy? We can't. Disclosing means risking, and because we risk we will sometimes fail.

Failure has become a heinous word in our culture. We are a nation of winners, and winning is defined in extremely rigid terms. If you watch the U.S. Open finals on television, the announcer will usually describe just two people: the winner and the loser—even though the "loser" beat hundreds of other contestants to arrive at the final match.

This narrow point of view overlooks one very important fact of life: No one can become a winner without losing many, many times. Lee Iacocca became a popular symbol of success *only* after suffering catastrophic failures. Walt Disney created Mickey Mouse in tribute to the very real mouse who skittered across his floors and shared his suppers during days of grinding poverty. And batting champions like Babe Ruth still hold the dubious distinction of striking out more often than other players.

In order to become willing to take risks of your own, it's important to understand what you're trying to protect yourself from. Having a concrete idea of your fears will keep them in proportion; letting them lurk in the dark will allow them to grow to overwhelming proportions.

People fear to disclose themselves for many reasons. Here are some of the most common ones. Do any of them sound familiar? If not, take the time to cut your own fears down to size by putting them into words.

- I am afraid of losing control.
- I am afraid of appearing weak and pitiable.
- I am afraid of seeing things about myself that I do not want to see.
- I am afraid of being abandoned.
- I am afraid of being misunderstood.
- I am afraid of being challenged by another.
- I am afraid of discovering a problem I will not be able to solve.

- I am afraid of becoming dependent on someone.
- I am afraid of someone becoming dependent upon me.
- I am afraid of losing respect for myself.
- I am afraid of becoming trapped.
- I am afraid of discovering a need that will be difficult to fill.

Learning to Disclose

The secretive person is hampered by old, ingrained behavior patterns. She has learned how to isolate herself from others and how to withhold herself, but she has never learned how to share herself with others.

It's important to understand that self-disclosure is a social skill, not a mysterious rite. Like all social skills, it can be learned, practiced, and improved on. Listed here are six conditions necessary for making successful disclosure.

1. *Honesty.* Self-disclosure means revealing something real and genuine about yourself to another. It doesn't mean distracting yourself or the other person with hypothetical problems and theatrics. Some people have become remarkable actors, churning out high-intensity disclosures that spell significance with a capital *S.* Often, these disclosures are shamelessly self-congratulatory. The would-be writer who never writes, for example, often *confesses* to a fear of success. This is mere stage dressing for the genuine problem—a deep-seated fear of failure.

Dishonest disclosures do a great deal of harm. They keep the discloser from coming to grips with real issues by throwing up a smoke screen of phony concerns. They also deepen isolation and alienation. The person on the receiving end senses that he is being used and the relationship quickly stagnates.

2. *Someone to disclose to.* Someone doesn't mean just anyone. In order to make successful disclosures, you must pick an appropriate other to disclose to. A person can be inappropriate for any number of reasons. Someone you work for or someone who works for you is often too involved in your business life to be a good candidate. Also a poor candidate is the person whose time, understanding, or willingness to listen are severely limited. The worst choice of all is the person who listens for ulterior motives—to play armchair psychologist or engage in a game of confessional one-upmanship. Intimacy does not just depend on your ability to disclose—it also depends upon the person who receives that disclosure.

3. *A sense of time and place.* Many people engage in disclosures without regard to anything else that's happening around them. The woman who unburdens herself to a new acquaintance is likely to frighten that person away, closing the door on future intimacy. The husband who attempts to discuss an important issue with a wife who's harried and exhausted is likely to meet with disappointment.

Just as there are appropriate and inappropriate people to disclose to, there are appropriate and inappropriate opportunities in which to make disclosures. The person who pays no attention to this is either woefully self-absorbed or subconsciously trying to thwart the intimacy she thinks she's seeking.

4. *A spontaneous approach.* The open person does

not approach an encounter bent on self-revelation. She has no set speech in mind and no well-rehearsed life history on her lips. Disclosing oneself doesn't mean aggressively explaining who you are and what you're all about. Rather, openness is the absence of defensiveness. It is the ability to be yourself in the presence of another. It's important to remember that not all disclosures are made with words. Spontaneous actions and reactions often speak volumes, where studied words would only interfere.

5. *Reasonable expectations.* What do you expect to get in return for sharing yourself with another? Healthful and productive disclosures are made without high price tags. Of course, you hope that the person you disclose to will be receptive and empathetic, but expectations that go beyond that are likely to meet with disappointment.

The person who repeatedly feels cheated or let down after making disclosures may be filled with unrealistic expectations. She may expect the other person to become responsible for her problems, to take them on as if they were her own. Or she may hope that the other person will make a personal commitment of love or support. Expectations like this fall into the realm of game-playing: *I'll disclose myself in order to get this or that in return.* This thinking is self-sabotaging. It loses sight of the fact that self-disclosure is a worthy goal in and of itself.

6. *Receptivity.* Intimacy does not happen all at once. It develops slowly, through the ritual of sharing. As intimacy grows, people make increasingly significant disclosures to one another. At first the stakes are small—

you tell someone about the day you had, he tells you what his day was like. But as time goes on and disclosures are swapped back and forth, the stakes escalate. Soon you are sharing thoughts and feelings that are much more personal and self-revealing.

It's important that you learn to play both roles—the giver and the receiver. If you only know how to make disclosures but don't know how to receive them, you will thwart the ritual of sharing necessary for true intimacy.

Moving Ahead

Reading, reflecting, and gaining insight into one's problems are wonderful pastimes. But they don't amount to much unless you're able to put them to productive use. Deciding to become more open is one thing, but putting that decision to the test of action requires great courage.

Turning your life script around is difficult—as difficult as rechanneling the course of a river. In order to make lasting changes, you will need to arm yourself with four things: motivation, information, a plan of action, and patience.

• *Motivation* is the ingredient that makes all things possible. It enables people to overcome great obstacles and triumph against the odds. Too often, people lose sight of *why* they want to make changes. They go around feeling punished and rebellious, and soon they return to their old, comfortable behavior patterns.

Instead of giving yourself dead-end messages such as, "I must become more open," use statements such as, "I *choose* to be more open because. . . ." Remind yourself of the benefits that come with self-disclosure. This will boost your motivation and give you a positive goal to work toward.

- *Information.* Don't expect to have absorbed everything at once. If you feel foggy about certain points, go back and read those sections again. Try paraphrasing what you have read, using examples and insights from your own life to reinforce the concepts.

Although I have tried to give you useful information, it cannot match the information you have about yourself. Most people are quite capable of healing themselves. They know the answers to their questions, even though they're often unaware of it.

As you have read this, some answers about your own life have probably become clear to you. Pay attention to these newly discovered insights. If possible, spend some time writing about them—not just because they might slip away from you if you don't—but because writing itself will deepen your understanding.

- *A plan of action* is your blueprint for change. Saying that you are going to be more open is not enough. You must also decide what you are going to do to achieve that end. For example, if you have gone through life covering up something about yourself, you might decide to share that secret with another person. Or you might choose an easier first step. If you are prone to isolating yourself from others, you might choose something as simple as going to visit someone or asking someone out for coffee.

The plan you devise is up to you, and there are only two criteria needed to make the plan a successful one: first, that each step challenges you and, second, that each step moves you closer to your goal.

Remember, too, that plans can be experimented with. If you find yourself stuck in a certain point or find that something isn't working right, go back to the drawing board and start again.

- *Patience* is the ingredient most people forget. They're so anxious to get going that they expect everything to happen at once. Although psychologists occasionally speak about the "one-session" cure, this is extremely rare. Usually, even the most highly motivated individual has a difficult time changing.

It's important to remember that the behavior patterns of a lifetime do not vanish at the wink of an eye. Those patterns have come to pass because they serve a purpose. Over a period of time, they have become deeply ingrained habits.

If you expect change to come too quickly or too easily, you risk losing faith in the process and in yourself. You may become discouraged with yourself, question your ability to change, and give up on yourself completely.

As you are changing, you need to have patience with yourself. It will not always seem like you're making progress, and sometimes you won't be. At times you'll lose your footing and fall backward.

Think about how a baby learns to walk. The baby takes a step, totters and falls, only to pull himself up and begin again. Eventually, he learns to walk, not because each step was a success but because he is always ready to *try again.*

You can reach your goals in exactly the same way— by taking as many baby steps as you need to and always allowing yourself to try again.

PART II

Introduction

Lewis M. Andrews, Ph.D.

By now we've come to have a clearer understanding of where shame comes from and how it can undermine, not only our recovery from an addiction, but our capacity to lead a productive and well-balanced life in general. We've seen how factors as diverse as the attitudes of our parents and families, our religious upbringing, and our own abuse of substances all contribute to feelings of personal disgrace. We've also learned that our diminished opinion of ourselves can include harsh judgments that range from the very specific—such as negative attitudes about our bodies—to very vague and abstract conclusions about our lowly place in God's universe.

In the process, we've come to see that shame is not quite the same thing as guilt. Although both feelings involve severe self-judgment and reproach, guilt is the emotion we feel when we have harmed another person—cheated that person out of some money, failed to follow through on a commitment, or lied to gain a temporary advantage. Shame, on the other hand, is a sense of worthlessness we feel, independent of any damage we may have caused to others. To feel ashamed is to hold ourselves in contempt, not so much for what we have *done*, but because of who we *are*.

This distinction is an important one, not simply for intellectual reasons, but because it has profound implications for the healing of shame. If we are guilty, we can alleviate our pain by making some kind of amends—paying back the money we stole, for example, or simply saying "I'm sorry" to the person we insulted—if we feel shame, however, we must find a way to accept our essential self.

We've already encountered some very helpful ways to accomplish this, but our last two essays will be more specific. The first will focus directly on the use of the Twelve Steps of the Anonymous programs to overcome feelings of low esteem. The second will offer additional techniques suggested by the principles of Rational-Emotive Therapy. Together they offer genuine hope and relief for those of us who have too long been victims of the tyrant, shame.

The Twelve Steps and Shame

Mic Hunter

Mic Hunter is a licensed psychologist and a certified chemical dependency counselor with two degrees. He has had extensive experience in treating victims of childhood sexual abuse and is also the author of Abused Boys: The Neglected Victims of Sexual Abuse.

What Is Shame?

Shame is that burning in our faces when we think those around us have finally figured out how worthless we are. We think we're inadequate or worthless. It's when we hate to look anyone in the eye; when time seems to crawl and we wish we could disappear. It makes us feel hopeless, helpless, and empty. Someone has seen our real self and we're sure they're disgusted.

We all have basic needs including food, water, shelter, touch, attention, and sleep. When any of our needs is repeatedly paired with a shaming experience we become shame-based. As a result, each time we have one of these needs we feel shame. For example, people with eating disorders have been shamed for needing food. "You're eating again," a man says to his partner. "You're a pig. How can anyone love you when you look like that? You make me sick." A compulsive cycle has begun. Each time this person wants to eat, he or she will feel shameful about it; and each time she feels shame she will think of eating.

Once we've become shame-based, the shame is self-triggering. Each time someone pays attention to us, even in a positive way, we feel ashamed.

How a Twelve Step Program Works

What is it about the Twelve Steps that brings people relief? The power of the Steps comes from addressing the dynamics of shame, which is at the core of many compulsive behaviors. Addicts, however, don't have an exclusive claim on shame. Everybody has shame, but we addicts have more than our fair share. Many of us were once children in addictive families, where rules supported and even encouraged addictive behavior. The addiction can be to using alcohol, other drugs, food, or sex, or to other compulsive behaviors. Whatever the addiction, families with addictions are shame-based.

This means rules are reinforced in a shaming way. When we broke the rules we were shamed. Rather than being told we did a bad thing, we were told we were a bad person. For example, a child at dinner spills milk. The parent says, "You're nothing but a *milk spiller*. You always spill your milk. Nobody could love a *milk spiller*. You should be ashamed of yourself." Now the child has been labeled a milk spiller and told she is unlovable. There's no way to redeem herself since she "always" spills her milk. Even after she cleans up the milk she'll still think of herself as a *milk spiller*. Finally, the parent pours her half a glass of milk, reminding her that she is a milk spiller and can't be trusted with a full glass.

Years go by and the child becomes an adult. But still she subconsciously thinks of herself as that *milk spiller*. If she has children, she will likely pour them half a glass of milk too, since, no doubt, they will also be milk spillers. If this sounds familiar, then you know what shame is.

What Twelve Step groups do is help us change our shame-based identity into a guilt-based identity. That's right, *guilt*. Guilt has gotten a bad name, because people have confused it with shame. Guilt is the emotion that helps us learn, and stay within our value system. If we do something bad, it's proper, even desirable, to feel guilty. For instance, when I behave in a way that violates one of my values I feel guilty. That motivates me to seek the person harmed and make amends. Then my guilt goes away, because it's no longer needed. (If we feel bad or can't seem to forgive ourselves long after we've made amends, chances are we aren't feeling guilty; more likely it's shame.)

Guilt also prevents us from behaving in ways that will cause us more guilt. I know if I do certain things I'll feel guilty. And since I don't want to feel guilty I'll more than likely avoid that behavior.

Shame and Guilt

Let's return to the example of the child who spilled milk. In a *guilt-based* family the parents would tell her that spilling milk is messy, wastes food, and disrupts mealtime, and that they get angry when she spills. The parents may also add that a way to deal with making a mess is to clean it up. The child has now learned that milk spilling is frowned on, and she can make amends by cleaning up the milk. Very likely, in the future she'll be more careful. Guilt-based families make three things clear:

- mistakes are part of being human;
- a mistake is only a mistake, not a reflection of someone's personal worth;
- damage can be repaired and forgiveness received.

Shame and Recovery

With any addiction there's more to recovery than stopping compulsive behaviors and thoughts. Alcoholics Anonymous has recognized this for years. As some say, "There's more to it than puttin' the plug in the jug." Alcoholics who merely stop drinking and don't work a recovery program never seem to find a comfortable sobriety or serenity. They're commonly referred to as "dry drunks." Having a fairly superficial understanding of the First Step, they stop their alcohol use. But they don't see the need for working the other Steps. By not working the remaining eleven Steps they often remain shameful and unhappy. Frequently, a person will go so far as to stop one addictive behavior, such as using drugs, only to begin acting compulsively with something else. The something else may be food, caffeine, tobacco, sex, or gambling. This is because the root of the problem—the shame—has not been addressed.

Feeling shame is like having a hole in our soul. Compulsive behavior attempts to fill this hole, but without success. If we dislike ourselves before getting drunk, we'll still dislike ourselves when we're drunk and when we sober up. Likewise, people with self-hate can eat or masturbate compulsively to find relief, but their self-hate remains. The compulsive behavior only serves to briefly numb their pain.

Step One: Admitting Our Powerlessness

We admitted we were powerless over (problem)—that our lives had become unmanageable.*

When we begin recovery in a Twelve Step program it's important for us to "act as if." If we wait until we think we're worthy of a support group and nurturing experiences, we may never get around to beginning our recovery. We need to act as if we deserve kind treatment. As we behave differently, we begin to feel and think differently. And then we *are* different. Our new,

---

* Adapted from the First Step of Alcoholics Anonymous, which reads, "We admitted we were powerless over alcohol—that our lives had become unmanageable." The complete Twelve Steps of AA are reprinted at the back of this book.

healthier attitudes and behaviors will begin to seem natural.

A ritual introduction is one technique that Twelve Step meetings use to reduce shame. Frequently, meetings start with someone saying, "Hello, I'm Jackie [or whoever] and I'm an addict." The dreaded secret is out. But no one runs screaming from the room; everyone looks at her and says, "Hi, Jackie!" She has begun a relationship with a roomful of people, and her shame has started decreasing.

Another way we can lessen our shame is when we "tell our story." In a First Step meeting, we tell about our addiction, what happened, and what it is like now. We might feel shameful. But we start to heal because nobody leaves while we are feeling shame. A relationship begins between us and our listeners. Further, people make comments such as, "I know what that's like. I did that too." We no longer feel alone in facing this challenge.

Having a Sense of Control

Once we admit we're out of control we may begin having a sense of control. Powerlessness means that as practicing addicts we didn't have a choice in our behavior. Our addiction forced us to behave the way we did. If we believe that we chose to act the way we did, hurting ourselves and others, we'll feel shameful. What kind of people would willfully hurt themselves and others? Only bad people, seems the logical answer. But if we believe we behaved harmfully because of our addiction, then we're still acceptable people and deserve recovery—and help from other recovering addicts. The choice is ours. Remember, though, that even if our behavior resulted from our addiction, we're still responsible for our actions.

When we're attending a Twelve Step group, we have others to help us in stopping the compulsive behavior coming from our addictions. With some addictions, such as chemical dependency, the recovery goal is abstinence. In others, such as sex, eating, spending, and work, the goal is moderation, which can be more difficult. Moderation is tough for addicts who tend to live in extremes. Working the Steps helps us find balance. Extreme behaviors and attitudes become less attractive. When people talk about serenity, they're talking about living a life of balance.

One way to balance our lives is to admit our powerlessness to control our world. All of us, whether we are addicts or not, are powerless to control some things, no matter how hard we try.

People who grow up in shame-based families or churches, or work for shame-based companies, don't usually know about powerlessness. They tend to assume that if something doesn't turn out the way it should, an outcome isn't what they wanted, it's their fault because they didn't try hard enough. They don't know that there are some things they can control, and some they can't. I hear that often when I listen to people in recovery:

- "I shouldn't need help with this."
- "If I just tried harder, I know I could control this."

- "If I were a real man I could handle this problem on my own."
- "I don't need a group. I don't want to burden them with my problems. I can handle it."

The First Step also introduces us to the idea of unmanageability. People with too much shame are bound to have unmanageable lives. That's because the rules in shame-based families make you feel you're damned if you do, damned if you don't. It's no wonder we feel shame.

We can feel shame from conditional relationships. When someone treats us in a shaming manner, the implication is that our relationship with them is conditional, we've failed as a person, and aren't worthy of the relationship. This can lead us to emotional, spiritual, and sometimes physical isolation. To recover from shame, we need to remove the isolation barrier and build in its place supportive and accepting relationships.

Whenever I have clients who regularly attend Twelve Step groups but who don't seem to be making progress on reducing shame, I ask them to quote the First Step. Frequently, their response is, "Admitted I am powerless . . ." I often stop them there, saying, "It sounds like you forgot the most important word, the WE, as in 'we admitted we were powerless . . .' Perhaps you've overlooked the key to the program. Maybe that's one reason you're struggling." Typically, these people are trying to recover alone, which is difficult and unnecessary. Remember, the Twelve Step program was founded on one addict helping him- or herself by helping others. It's one of the reasons the Steps work.

Sponsorship helps for the same reason. A sponsor may say, "Your recovery matters. You matter. I'm here because you're worth knowing and helping." This is hard to accept if we're shame-based people to whom even positive attention triggers shame. It may seem easier to do without a sponsor, to try to slip in and out of meetings unnoticed, or to have a sponsor in name only and never develop a real relationship.

Step Two: Restoring Our Sanity

Came to believe that a Power greater than ourselves could restore us to sanity.

Our shame may tell us that we're bad, have always been bad, and will always be bad. The Second Step addresses this by challenging the belief that we can't change our behaviors. It can be interpreted to mean that our shame-based identity is abnormal and was inflicted on us. It's not our true self.

Nearly anyone with a shame-based identity knows that shame can seem overwhelming, bigger than anyone or anything. The Second Step offers the possibility of having a relationship with a more gentle "Power greater than ourselves." In this way, our belief in a Higher Power helps us rather than handicaps us.

Step Three: In a Higher Power's Care

Made a decision to turn our will and our lives over to the care of God as we understood Him.

To heal shame, we need relationships. The Third Step addresses this by helping us form a trusting relationship with a Higher Power of our understanding. This is hard for many of us because shame has taught us we don't deserve quality relationships, let alone a relationship with God.

A second barrier can be the confusion between our experience with our parents and our concept of God. When we were infants our parents may have been godlike to us. If they treated us in a shaming manner, however, we probably grew up to believe that God is like that too. We may be afraid of God or think we have no use for spirituality. But spirituality can help heal the isolation of shame by providing us with a sense of connection—we begin to feel we have a place in the universe and an inherent worth.

A third barrier to using this Step is "institutionalized" shame. Many families seem to believe that shaming children enough will make them change. This belief in the power of shaming to change behavior is also held by some churches, schools, companies, and even therapists. Usually, however, shaming people in hopes of making them better doesn't work. They usually behave worse, and may get another dose of shame. If we've had hurtful experiences in shame-based institutions, the Third Step will help us change to gain shame-free spirituality.

Step Four: Making an Inventory

Made a searching and fearless moral inventory of ourselves.

When we work the First Step in a group, with our sponsor, or in treatment, we reduce the shame we feel about our addiction. Part of this process is writing down examples of the ways we've tried to control or stop compulsive behaviors that caused our lives to be unmanageable. We find other addicts have similar behaviors. In the Fourth Step we take a broader look at our lives. This Step can help us improve our relationship with ourselves. It helps us answer the question, *Who am I?* We are more than addicts. We are more than spouses, employees, parents, or any other label. The Fourth Step helps us look, not only at what we do, but who we are. Our shame would try to convince us that if we took a good look at ourselves we'd see how bad we are. The Fourth Step is a time to learn that our worth as a person can withstand intense scrutiny. *We are acceptable.*

The "Problem Statement" for another Twelve Step group, Adult Children of Alcoholics, deals with looking at ourselves. It contains the sentence, "We have an overdeveloped sense of responsibility and it is easier for us to be concerned with others rather than ourselves; this enables us not to look too closely at our faults or our responsibility to ourselves." Clearly, anyone who relates to that phrase would benefit from a Fourth Step. A moral inventory may cause us to pay attention to ourselves.

If we approach Step Four with shame, we might magnify our faults and reduce our assets. It is hard for people with much shame to think they might have many positive traits. An inventory needs to contain both our strengths and weaknesses to keep us thinking positively.

Step Five: Admitting Our Shortcomings

Admitted to God, to ourselves, and to another human being the exact nature of our wrongs.

The Fifth Step gives us a chance to share ourselves with another person and with our Higher Power. The Steps point out our need to have others in our lives if we're to heal. Taking an inventory of ourselves isn't enough. It needs to be shared with another person.

The Fifth Step also helps us challenge the belief system of shame. Shame causes us not to let anyone see our true self. Purposely sharing ourselves with God and another person is a very powerful, shame-reducing experience. Even after we've worked the First Step and been accepted by others it's easy to hold on to shame. *Oh sure, you accept me after what I've done, but you have to—you've done similar things. You're addicts too. Normal people couldn't understand or accept me.* Believing that we're worthwhile to some people is a good start; learning and believing that we're acceptable, period, is even better.

With this in mind, it may be wise to do our Fifth Step with someone who shares our addiction. After some time in stable recovery, though, we may find it useful to do additional Fifth Steps with people from other backgrounds. This helps us gain acceptance from all types of people. For example, we might seek someone with a different religion, race, gender, economic, or educational background.

Step Six: Removing Character Defects

Were entirely ready to have God remove all these defects of character.

The Sixth Step provides us with hope. It implies that our shame can be removed. Our shame, however, would have us believe that we were born flawed, will always be flawed, and there's no hope for being worthwhile. Step Six says that this flaw—which we believe to be in the core of our being—can be removed. To some people, this can be a frightening thought. *If I am not the rotten person I thought I was—then who am I?*

We might have tried for years to remove our defects, but have had few satisfying results. Perhaps we've blamed this lack of progress on laziness, stupidity, or weak will. But as with so many of the Steps, the Sixth Step points out that recovery is a team effort and reminds us that being human means not being able to function alone. When we ask our Higher Power to help change our character, we'll likely find more gratifying results than from our solo attempts.

The Desire for Perfection

When some people read the Sixth Step, they feel shameful again. They think, *Oh no, I'm doing it wrong. I'm not totally, absolutely ready. So I must be a bad person, and therefore, I'll never recover.* That kind of perfectionism is a sign of shame. Some shameful people believe, *If I do everything perfectly, nobody will notice that I'm a no-good person.* That thinking won't work. It's flawed because people *never* do anything perfectly. And so the person thinks, *Well, I failed, therefore, I'm no good as a person.* They try even harder to be perfect and the compulsive cycle continues.

Addiction is about extremes. For example, compulsive eating is one extreme, while compulsive non-eating (anorexia nervosa) is equally destructive. Since addiction is drastic, many people think that recovery would be too. Many of us addicts have lived selfish lives. So when we begin the recovery process, we may think we should go to the opposite extreme and become self*less*. We may put others' needs first and never consider what is important to ourselves. This is inappropriate, as well as painful, and we finally get fed up and angry. Neither extreme is enjoyable. The ideal is self-respect. This is when our wants and needs matter just as much as others' wants and needs. Recovery is gaining this kind of balance and moderation in life.

Step Seven: Removing Our Shortcomings

Humbly asked Him to remove our shortcomings.

As shameful people, we tend to think, feel, and behave in extremes. Everything is yes/no, right/wrong, and all/nothing. We rarely use words like "moderation" and "balance." Humility is a hard concept for us to grasp.

Humility is understanding that we're worthwhile. We need not compare ourselves with others. Self-worth is not a contest. Humble people don't value themselves too much or too little. They also don't over- or under-value others. Humility is that middle ground between the extremes of grandiosity and intense shame. We aren't less of a person than others, nor are we better than other people. It doesn't matter what kind of title or job we have, what we own, or how much money, fame, and schooling we have. Our house may be better than someone else's, but our self isn't better than theirs.

Some shameful people use grandiosity to try to reassure themselves that they're acceptable. Grandiose people lack closeness since they must insulate themselves from the risk of being criticized. They won't listen to helpful advice because their self-worth is based on being perfect. Caught up in grandiosity, they are so alert for any sign of criticism they tend to find it even when it doesn't exist. For example, I say to someone, "I noticed that you got your hair cut."

"So what," she snaps back. "Are you saying it doesn't look good?"

"No," I reply. "I like it better than your old style."

"So now you're saying that I was ugly before I got my haircut, is that it?" No matter what's said, shame-filled people may take it as an attack.

Since humility doesn't require comparisons, humble people aren't intimidated by others' advice or their qualities. For example, you being lovable and acceptable doesn't take away from me being equally lovable and acceptable. There's enough to go around. But to hide their limitations, shaming parents create the myth of shortages. People who tell me that they don't need anyone usually come from families where no one was there emotionally. People who say their feelings are "too big" likely had parents who didn't know what to do when their children were emotional.

One sign of humility is the ability to laugh about ourselves and our actions. Notice I said *about* rather than *at* ourselves. Holding ourselves up for ridicule in the name of humor is a sign of shame, not humility.

We can laugh about ourselves when we see that we're acceptable people. Our occasional floundering proves we're human. Humble people don't have to take themselves so seriously because they accept their self-worth. Laughing together, when it's not at anyone's expense, brings people together. When Twelve Step meetings are working, healthy laughter is common.

Step Eight: Making the List

> *Made a list of all people we had harmed, and be-*
> *came willing to make amends to them all.*

We can use patience to help heal us as victims of shame. The Twelve Steps are written so that a preparation Step precedes an action Step. For example, Step Two prepares us for taking action in Step Three. So it is with Steps Eight and Nine.

In Step Eight, we review our lives and take an inventory of the wrongs we've done—without having to face anyone immediately. Shame-bound people may think of past bad behaviors and brand themselves bad. This shame response, however, prevents them from making amends and healing wounded relationships. And a lack of relationships leads to isolation and more shame.

It's difficult for shame-based people to face others. We need to reduce shame before meeting with those we have hurt. Working the first seven Steps reduces shame in several ways. In the First Step, we learned that some of our behavior was due to powerlessness. The Second and Third Steps gave us a Higher Power to rely on. The Fourth and Fifth Steps offered a chance to expose our shame to another person and be accepted. The Sixth and Seventh Steps helped us remove our character defects and accept ourselves and our inherent worth. These Steps combine to convert our high level of shame into a lower level of guilt, which is more manageable. When we're ready to work on the Eighth Step, we are less likely to be shameful or to avoid people. Guilt is more likely to motivate us to try to make amends.

When making our amends list, and thinking about how we've harmed others, we might consider intent. Did we intend to hurt others by our actions? Most times the answer is no. This insight often greatly reduces shame.

Step Nine: Making Direct Amends

Made direct amends to such people wherever possible, except when to do so would injure them or others.

Since shame often results from broken relationships, in healing we may want to nurture relationships. Shame attempts to teach us that we aren't worthy, or that what we've done is so horrible that it's unforgivable. The Ninth Step gives us a chance to prove that idea wrong. Taking genuine responsibility for an inappropriate act reduces our shame. The Ninth Step further suggests that we also might seek those persons we have wronged and add something positive to the relationship. Amend means "to add to." The Step doesn't speak of apologies. Working the Ninth Step is a gift to ourselves, not something that we give to others.

Self-forgiveness is often difficult for people who have felt shameful for a long time. When making direct amends we're often surprised that others have forgiven us long before we're willing to forgive ourselves. A common block to effectively working this Step is grandiosity. Or we may believe we're the most unworthy being in the universe whom not even God can find forgivable.

The Ninth Step encourages us to seek out people to make amends "except when to do so would hurt them or others." This keeps us from causing even more shame in ourselves and others. If an overwhelming level of shame still haunts us after working the preceding eight Steps, we may want to postpone making face-to-face amends and repeat the Fourth and Fifth Steps. Or we might consider seeking help from a professional who understands treating shame-based people.

Step Ten: Ongoing Personal Inventory

Continued to take personal inventory and when we were wrong promptly admitted it.

The first nine Steps have helped us to convert our unwanted shame into useful guilt, and to relieve that guilt. The remaining Steps outline a maintenance program to keep us guilt-based, rather than shame-based.

Shame makes us seek perfection to try to cover up what we see as our worthlessness. The Tenth Step, however, makes no such demands. The wording of Step Ten isn't "*if* we were wrong," but "*when* we were wrong." The word *when* permits us to be wrong. We can make mistakes and still be acceptable. This Step teaches what to do when we make a mistake: promptly admit it, whether to ourselves or another person. Promptly admitting means that we're less likely to dwell on the mistake or use it to prove that we aren't good people. In working the Tenth Step we admit that our behavior was an error and let it go at that.

Shame-based people may have a habit of feeling bad even when they haven't done anything wrong. The Tenth Step helps reduce this tendency. It asks us to only be accountable for what we've done or not done that was our responsibility. We're not expected to atone for all of humanity's wrongs. The Tenth Step is especially important in the recovery of adult children of alcoholics and those in Al-Anon, who often feel guilty for someone else's behavior.

Step Eleven: Improving Our Spirituality

Sought through prayer and meditation to improve our conscious contact with God as we understood Him, *praying only for knowledge of His will for us and the power to carry that out.*

It's difficult to discuss shame without also discussing spirituality. A shame-based identity often exists without spirituality. Spirituality is the sense that we're a part of something bigger and somehow connected. Shame requires isolation and a belief of uniqueness.

In the Fifth Step we shared ourselves with a Higher Power. The Eleventh Step asks that we keep doing this daily. Many shame-based people grow up rarely interacting with God. Or if they do it's not a genuine relationship. For example, they may only pray when in trouble. The Eleventh Step, by contrast, urges us to have a personal relationship with God. This means talking and listening as we would in any other significant relationship. Prayer is talking to God; meditation is listening for God to speak. When we have an ongoing personal relationship with our Higher Power it increases our spirituality and reduces our shame. This allows us to stop acting grandiosely, chasing after perfection, and playing God. Instead, we're free to relax and enjoy being human.

For those of us using our group as our Higher Power, the same holds true. Going to meetings is one of our spiritual experiences. When we listen at meetings we are meditating, and when we speak we are praying. Going to meetings and remaining superficial not only doesn't reduce shame, but may increase it.

I've known several people with this problem. They went to meetings regularly, but did little to bare their souls. They rarely called people during the week. They offered help but never asked for support. The longer they went to meetings the more shameful they became. They saw other people who had attended meetings for less time getting close to others and liking themselves. They began to see this as proof that they were different from others, or somehow so damaged that even the Twelve Steps couldn't help. Finally, however, they began to share their pain with their sponsors who urged them to develop more personal relationships with other group members. Thus, they found relief.

Step Twelve: Practicing the Principles

*Having had a spiritual awakening as the result of these steps, we tried to carry this message to other addicts and to practice these principles in all our affairs.**

If we're shame-based, shame reaches into every aspect of our lives. It colors our view of self, sex, emotions, others, and God. Fortunately, recovery, too, affects every aspect of life.

As recovering people, we can be role models for addicts who still suffer. Helping others lower their shame level helps us to reduce our shame. By offering help, we show others that we think they're worthwhile as people and that they're worthy of recovery. Our offering help is a way to say to ourselves and to others that we are worthwhile people with something of value to give.

For our shame to heal, we need these relationships. If we only associate with others recovering from the same addiction, we may reduce some of our shame, but only some. To fully recover we need as part of our support network, people who don't have our addiction—ideally, people who don't have any addiction. This helps us shatter the myth that only people like us can understand and accept us. Part of "prac-

* Adapted from Step Twelve of Alcoholics Anonymous, which reads "Having had a spiritual awakening as the result of these steps, we tried to carry this message to alcoholics, and to practice these principles in all our affairs."

ticing these principles in all our affairs'' is to practice our new behaviors with people who aren't addicts.

As you can see, the Twelve Step program provides an easily accessible, no-cost environment for healing from too much shame. The framework and support system it offers allows us to reduce our self-defeating behaviors and increase self-respect. The changes we can make within this system are profound and lasting. It's a valuable resource for all of us, whether we are addicts or not.

Rational-Emotive Therapy for Shame: Your Personal Power to Change

Tim Sheehan, Ph.D.

Tim Sheehan, Ph.D., is a licensed consulting psychologist with fourteen years of experience working with people with emotional and addiction problems. He has conducted workshops on dual diagnosis, heads the psychology department at the Hazelden Foundation, and is an adjunct associate professor at St. Mary's College of Minnesota.

Understanding our feelings is no easy task. Most of us have felt the burden of shame at one time or another. Some of us may have been dishonest about our feelings—to ourselves and others—for fear we would be found out or others would know too much. Hurtful feel-

"Rational-Emotive Therapy for Shame: Your Personal Power to Change" is from *Rational-Emotive Therapy—Shame: Discover Your Personal Power to Change* by Tim Sheehan, Ph.D. Reprinted, with changes, by permission of Hazelden Foundation. ©1989, 1992 by Hazelden Foundation. All rights reserved. The second edition (1992) appears in this volume.

The ABC process described in this chapter is based on the work of Albert Ellis and his Rational-Emotive Therapy.

ings frequently surface in recovery, and when we hurt, we feel bad. Words like *miserable* or *sad* can describe these hurtful feelings. Sometimes we not only *feel* bad, we believe we *are* bad. We not only hurt, we also believe something is wrong with the very core of us. We believe something is wrong not only with our use of alcohol or other drugs, but with the core of who we are. We feel something is lacking—we feel inadequate and empty.

That pervasive feeling of chronic emptiness is often *shame*. The void is deepened by self-reproach and a constant longing to be filled. The void of shame is a trap in recovery that robs us of contentment and makes not using alcohol or other drugs or refraining from binge eating and other compulsive behaviors seem impossible.

For most of us, shame has its roots in our childhood. Addiction and emotional problems run in families, and many of us were raised in unhealthy families that did not function well at meeting our emotional, and sometimes our physical needs. When parents are chronically depressed or overwhelmed in their struggle with an alcohol or other drug dependency, they are often unable to meet the emotional needs of their children. When children do not get their emotional needs met, they often feel shame.

A nurturing family naturally provides for each member's emotional needs. Children are accepted for who they are; they are cared for and respected. The individuality of family members is maintained. Parents are free to be adults, and children are free to be children.

Shame is fostered when a child's emotional needs are not met, when that child is not allowed to grow as a valuable person free to explore personal strengths, test individual limits, and embrace himself or herself emotionally.

Shame grows when children and adolescents feel abandoned or neglected, when they are not given adequate care to grow and develop and to value themselves as worthwhile people. These children and adolescents often mature with deeply entrenched beliefs of inadequacy and worthlessness.

Inadequate nurturing during childhood can take a number of different forms. For some of us it was blatant:

- being hit, pushed, or slapped
- being coerced into sexual behavior
- being abandoned for days at a time

For many of us, it was subtle and pervasive:

- being compared with high-achieving brothers and sisters
- being subjected to derogatory remarks about our masculinity or femininity
- being criticized about our ability to achieve or make it on our own
- being criticized about our appearance or weight
- being constantly reminded of mistakes we made
- being threatened that we would turn out just like our "no-good drunken father"

People raised with inadequate nurturing often learn to be vigilant around others lest someone else discover their feelings of inadequacy. They may feel a need to hide themselves, their emotions, and their thoughts. It becomes important to them to keep secrets, to resist discovery, to avoid making mistakes. Mistakes are seen as the ultimate evidence of worthlessness. A mistake is not viewed as an isolated event, but it is generalized to describe the entire self: *I am a mistake. My shame means that I not only* feel *bad, but that I believe I am* bad, inadequate, and flawed.

This sort of reasoning promotes a vicious cycle where children who aren't valued often mature to adulthood believing they are not valuable. To hide their feelings of worthlessness, they develop a rigid defense system. No one is to find out about them. Hints of inadequacy are cautiously guarded. They deny and distrust their emotions and no longer freely express their feelings, show affection, or feel comfortable with their sexuality. Chronic unhappiness, apathy, and anticipation of being found out take the place of feelings of trust and sharing.

Shame and Chemical Dependency

Shame can also be learned later in life. Those of us who struggle with a drug addiction can despair over our emotional problems as the addictive cycle escalates and eventually defeats our attempts to lead a healthier, more productive life. Robbed of our feelings of hope, this self-defeating cycle only underscores our behavior problems and exaggerates our feelings of worthlessness.

Self-Defeating Behavior

Ellen has been drug- and alcohol-free for the last six months, yet she is overwhelmed by chronic feelings of emptiness and self-doubt. She feels paralyzed and can't identify or express her feelings. She fears that her lack of worth will be transparent. She no longer has her pills and alcohol to fill the void. For self-protection, Ellen relies on a rigid defense mechanism, and vows to herself that no one will learn of her feelings of utter worthlessness and shame; no one will know her secret. Instead, Ellen strives to be "perfect."

Ellen's reliance on perfectionism is a frequently used defense against shame. Perfectionism is actually a rigid belief system, "a judge within," that monitors, evaluates, and critiques our behavior, thoughts, and feelings. The judge within demands perfection. Mistakes are disastrous! We think we must achieve in all areas of our lives to be worthwhile. We convince ourselves that only a perfect performance will compensate for our inward feelings of shame.

Ellen is caught between two unrealistic demands: her never-ending and impossible striving for perfect behavior, and her insistence that she keep her shameful feelings secret. She is in a no-win situation. Although Ellen has stopped using pills, her shame continues to motivate perfectionistic behaviors that limit her ability to seek the help she so desperately needs.

Jim is haunted by a nagging feeling of inadequacy. Outwardly, he projects an image of self-confidence. Inwardly, however, he feels incomplete. He secretly takes one drink after another in a futile effort to quell his addiction, fill his persistent feelings of emptiness, and quiet his feelings of shame. The more he tries to numb his feelings, the emptier he feels. Self-defeating behavior dulls our pain or helps us feel good momentarily, but it doesn't solve any of our problems.

Jim's addiction seems—at least temporarily—to fill the void of shame. But like Ellen, who relies on perfectionism to mask her shame, Jim eventually deepens his feelings of worthlessness by drinking. Jim's alcoholism actually dulls his perception of shame. Both Jim's and Ellen's responses to shame are self-defeating. Jim's dependence on alcohol dulls the pain of shame but only for a time. Ellen avoids her feelings of shame but defeats her purpose of getting help for her emotional turmoil by maintaining a rigid facade of perfectionism.

Shame and Its Self-Defeating Consequences

Shame is an emotional problem. Emotions are problems when they block us from reaching some of our most basic goals. For many of us, building a more healthy lifestyle involves developing fulfilling relationships by allowing ourselves to be vulnerable and imperfect with those we trust and accepting the vulnerability and imperfections of others. To be human is to be fallible and less than perfect. Recovery also means actively participating in the world of work, taking joy in living day to day, and, of course, remaining abstinent. When a feeling such as shame blocks us from fulfilling one of these basic tasks, we have an emotional problem.

Shame is therefore an obstacle to learning the basic tasks of living. Feelings of chronic emptiness can undermine our efforts to feel content and can give us an excuse for relapse. Shame keeps us isolated and separated from others, thus sabotaging our needs for intimacy and meaningful relationships. It interferes with our capacity to relate to others as whole, imperfect persons.

Shame is a special problem for people recovering from addictions and emotional problems. If we have unidentified feelings of shame that are not dealt with, we are at risk for relapse. In fact, how we behave when we feel ashamed is often the opposite of how we behave in recovery. Recovery is the process by which we are restored to a more fulfilling life that often involves fewer emotional hardships and freedom from addictive behavior.

Characteristics of Shame	*Recovery Characteristics*
Seeks social isolation and emotional withdrawal.	Participates in the social process of recovery.
Feels lack of trust in oneself.	Trusts one's opinions and feelings.
Experiences constricted spontaneity.	Experiences joy.

Repeats similar mistakes.	Learns from past experience.
Relies on rigid behaviors.	Approaches problems with flexibility.

Since shame feels bad and results in our self-defeating behaviors, it is important that we identify and reduce our shame as part of our process of recovery.

Shame Versus Guilt

Shame is different from guilt. Guilt is a reactive feeling to a misbehavior, or an omission of an expected behavior. For example, an adolescent may feel guilty because he or she acted in ways that hurt others, or a father may feel guilty because he has neglected his son. Guilt is usually limited to a specific event and doesn't involve an evaluation of our basic worth as people. In fact, feelings of guilt are often healthy. They can be a signal to us that we've missed something or need to take a closer look at our behavior. We can learn to appreciate guilt, not fear it. It reminds us that we are imperfect, worthwhile humans able to learn from our mistakes and grow as fully functioning people.

In contrast, feelings of shame usually involve our sense of worth as people.

Shame is not a simple reaction to a specific event; rather, it is a learned emotional response that lingers no matter how good our performance might be.

When we feel shameful we are likely to isolate our-selves and to withdraw emotionally; we are less likely to be spontaneous and to feel joy. The self-defeating behaviors of shame reinforce unrelenting feelings of distress, emptiness, and worthlessness.

The Good News

Feelings of shame can be changed! Since shame is learned, it can be unlearned and replaced by more pos-itive attitudes, behaviors, and feelings. We can lessen our feelings of shame by understanding their roots, by acknowledging that we feel shame, and by consciously changing shame-related behaviors.

> Beliefs about our self, learned either early in child-hood or later in life, tend to persist even when our addiction has stopped.

As children, we tend to believe what adults teach us, particularly when these adults are considered trustwor-thy—such as parents, clergy, or teachers. As adoles-cents, we modify our attitudes based on our experiences. Thus, if we are faced with continued fail-ures, criticism, and our own early addictive behaviors, we soon learn to devalue our worth. Children and ad-olescents, by the nature of their youth, lack the neces-sary skills, knowledge, and emotional stability to understand the complexity of their attitudes and feel-ings. Consequently, we aren't responsible for how we were treated in the past or how we learned early on to feel about ourselves. In essence, we are not responsible

for our childhood. By nature, childhood is characterized by powerlessness.

The same is true for addiction and compulsive behaviors. Some of us have experienced obsessions and
compulsive behaviors that have invaded every part of
our personality; others of us have experienced a loss of
control over certain behaviors such as drinking or gambling. All of us have faced and felt the continued defeat
and destruction from our inability to change our behavior. Firm resolve and willpower alone have often resulted in dismal failure. Although we wanted the pain
of our self-defeating behavior to stop, we were powerless. Like children, we were powerless in our attempts
to control the complexities of our attitudes, feelings,
and addictive behavior.

It is only by accepting our powerlessness as adults
that we are empowered to recover. As recovering people, we are more aware of our feelings and can make
conscious choices about what we think and how we
behave. Shame is perpetuated by our belief systems. No
matter when, where, or how we learned them, these
shame-based attitudes are now our own. The judge
within who represents our perfectionistic strivings to
control can be disputed, diminished, and eventually
kicked off the bench! The judge's rule is not absolute
and can be diffused with persistent opposition based on
logic and reason.

RET Principles

While our shame may be rooted in the past, we need to cope with it in the present. One method to attack shame-based attitudes is to utilize a self-help approach: Rational-Emotive Therapy (RET). The premise of RET is that thoughts trigger feelings. Many of us think of our feelings as an automatic reaction to isolated events. We often talk about our uncomfortable feelings as if someone or something else were responsible for them: "She made me angry." Many of us believe that events at *A* cause emotions at *B*.

A	B
Events	*Feelings*

Feelings aren't automatic, however, nor are feelings necessarily similar or consistent in response to similar events. For instance, an event *(A)*, such as receiving feedback in a group, might result in a number of different feelings *(B)*, ranging from sadness to anger. So feelings vary from individual to individual and are not automatically linked to events. Thus, emotions are not directly caused by events. RET says that we can choose how to interpret or think about the event at B which in turn causes a feeling at *C*.

A	B	C
Event	*Thought*	*Feeling*
	Interpretation	

Ellen's Story

Although sober for six months, Ellen has been crippled by continual nightmares, sleepless nights, and relationship problems. She has sought the support of a women's therapy group. While she has mustered the courage to ask for help, she feels numb and unable to share her feelings. Ellen has relied for so long on a perfectionistic defense, keeping others at a safe distance, that it is now difficult to let others in.

Now journaling the events of her childhood, Ellen recalls a long-suppressed family history involving painful feelings and physical abuse. Both of Ellen's parents had been alcoholics. Ellen is filled with a surge of shame and subsequently dreads telling her story. As she thinks of her past, Ellen tells herself, I should have been able to stop the abuse. *I shouldn't have put up with it for so long. What an unlovable child I must have been to deserve such abuse. What an awful adult I've become. No one must know.*

A Event	B Thoughts	C Feelings	Behavioral Consequences
Telling the story.	I should have stopped the abuse.	shame	Isolated from peers, avoids telling her story.
	I shouldn't have put up with it.		

B
Thoughts
What an
unlovable
child I
must have
been.

What a
horrible
adult I've
become.

No one
must ever
know.

As a result of her shame, Ellen attempts to isolate herself in her group. Her behavior is self-defeating, since she eliminates the emotional support that she needs to face her secret. Ellen's belief system *(B)* is characterized by unrealistic demands further compounded by a tendency to ''awfulize'' herself. Ellen's ''should's'' and ''must's'' signify her unrealistic demands that she should have had more power or control. In turn, she debases her own worth by blaming herself and undermining her value as a person. Ellen interprets her past events through a filter of shame-inducing beliefs. The judge within formulates rigid expectations for Ellen's performance and shames her when she is unable to reach these unattainable goals.

Fortunately for Ellen, two of her peers helped to draw her out by sharing their stories in group. Eventually,

Ellen learned to dispute her shame-based logic *(D)* by raising such questions as *who? what?* and *why?*

B *Thoughts*	**C** *Feelings*	**D** *Critique*
I should have stopped the abuse.	shame	*Who* says I should have stopped the abuse? I was a child. I had no more power over my parents than they had over their drinking.
I shouldn't have had to put up with it.	shame	*What* choices did I have? Aren't we all powerless as children? I'm not responsible for my parents' behavior. Stop making unrealistic demands!
What an unlovable child I must have been.	shame	*What* evidence do I have that I was an unlov-

B Thoughts	C Feelings	D Critique
		table child? Aren't all children lovable and worthy? Aren't all children deserving of love and care?
What an awful adult I've become.	shame	Just because I was criticized in the past is no reason to criticize myself now. Sure, I'm not perfect, but who is? Aren't we all worthwhile, fallible humans?
No one must know.	shame	*Why?* I'm not responsible for my childhood. Aren't my parents responsible for their behavior? Because I was abused in the past is no proof that I am

B	**C**	**D**
Thoughts	*Feelings*	*Critique*
		a worthless
		adult now.

Setting Goals

As Ellen's logic begins to change, she is free to identify her goals. While her emptiness and shame will not
disappear overnight, she is more comfortable and less
upset more of the time. She has formulated a goal of
living a productive, healthy life with as little shame as
possible. To help reach her goals, Ellen is continuing
to participate in her women's therapy group and is beginning
individual therapy. In the meantime, Ellen is renewing her
emerging attitude of self-respect with an affirmation:

*I am Ellen, a fallible, worthwhile person deserving
of self-respect and the respect of others. Today I will
treat myself as a worthy, deserving person.*

Since Ellen's judge within is not easily disputed, she
has designed a concrete plan to help her use her new
affirmation. As a reminder, she pairs her self-affirmation
to a frequent daily activity. Since she drinks four sodas
each day, Ellen has decided to use her first sip as a cue
to repeat her positive affirmation. Once she completes
her self-affirmation, Ellen drinks the remainder of the
soda as a reward for her new attitude.

Later, Ellen draws up a list of shame-attacking activities with the help of her group therapist. While Ellen understands some of her shame-based attitudes, she also understands that her chronic feelings of emptiness could easily put her at risk for relapse into her old self-defeating behavior. Though she is feeling comfortable more of the time, she knows that her issues involving shame are not completely resolved.

Ellen has also decided to continue educating herself about shame. She has planned a special reading assignment, and she has found a therapist who is versed in both addiction and childhood abuse issues. Ellen plans to continue with her daily schedule of self-affirmations. Since she is also planning to attend her women's therapy group, Ellen has decided to complete at least two additional RET assignments so she will be better able to discuss her shame-based attitudes with her peers.

Ellen's shame is obviously rooted in childhood experiences, and her "awfulizing" attitudes about these experiences and about herself could have obstructed her progress. But by disputing her shaming logic, Ellen has empowered herself to make the changes she needs.

Jim's Story

In contrast, Jim's shame does not result from childhood experiences, but is instead directly related to the self-defeating consequences of addiction. The more he drinks, the less he values himself. Although he strives to control his drinking, his efforts are a dismal failure time after time. According to Jim, he should be able to control his drinking. Jim fervently believes that he is bad or worthless because he can't stop or reduce his drinking.

Jim can predict neither intervals of abstinence nor intoxication. He begins to see himself as a moral degenerate. Jim thinks if he had value or worth he would not degrade himself through continued intoxication and public humiliation. As Jim's shame mounts, he withdraws even further from his friends and family. He then drinks more in his isolation.

Jim's belief that he is worthless is based on his demand that he *should* be able to control his drinking. The judge within demands willpower and self-restraint and condemns Jim's worth when he is unable to control his behavior. Jim's shame and isolation are obstacles to his recovery—he shuts out all those who could be of help.

A Event	B Thoughts	C Feelings	Behavioral Consequences
Continued drinking.	I absolutely *should* be able to control my drinking.	shame	Social isolation, continued drinking.
	It's *awful* that I can't handle		

A	B	C	
Event	*Thoughts*	*Feelings*	*Behavioral Consequences*
	even one drink.		
	I'm simply a *bad* person.		

Jim's family and friends didn't give up. Through their support and understanding, Jim eventually agreed to treatment. However, the judge within continued to demand perfect control. Jim held onto his unrealistic demand that he should be able to control his drinking. Through concerted efforts from peers, and education regarding alcoholism, Jim began to dispute his logic at *(D)*.

B	C	D
Thoughts	*Feelings*	*Critique*
I absolutely should be able to control my drinking.	shame	Who says I should be able to control my drinking? Isn't alcoholism a disease? Disease is not a matter of will-power.

A	B	C	D
Event	*Thoughts*	*Feelings*	*Critique*
It's awful that I can't handle even one drink.	shame		Of course I can't handle just one drink. My drinking isn't a matter of voluntary control. Once I take one drink, I'm bound to finish the bottle.
I'm simply a *bad* person.	shame	Stop "awfulizing"! I have a bad disease. I am not a bad person.	

As Jim's beliefs about his alcoholism began to change, he became increasingly aware of his unrealistic demands of himself. In accepting his powerlessness over alcohol, Jim also accepted his own humanity with all its strengths and limitations.

Jim's shame is rooted in his belief that he needs to control the uncontrollable. For Jim to recognize his limitations as a human is an ongoing task—he is no longer striving to be perfect.

Taking Action

As Jim progressed, his counselor made a number of helpful recommendations. In order to reduce his shame, Jim needed to become more flexible in his expectations of himself and others. Since Jim had accepted himself as a fallible, worthwhile human, there was no longer any reason for him to listen to his judge within. His lack of control and powerlessness were no longer threats to his worth, but simply characteristics of being human. Any efforts to control the uncontrollable could only lead to failure and often to self-reproach and shame. With this in mind, Jim agreed to incorporate the following activities.

Finding a support group. Jim identified a need for ongoing support from a group that could help point out some of his shame-based thinking and self-defeating behavior. He understood that his attitudes often involved a need to control that easily sabotaged his acceptance of his alcoholism. Jim agreed to explore at least two different groups—AA and a men's support group.

Completing an RET assignment. Prior to his discharge from treatment, Jim also completed an additional RET assignment to dispute his demandingness, or what his counselor referred to as "shoulding." Jim learned that words such as *must* or *should* often represent unrealistic demands and are key words to dispute when changing attitudes. With this in mind, Jim began to work on his RET assignment on feelings of shame that related to his marriage.

Jim wrote down "shame" as an emotional problem under *C* (feelings). Jim knew that his feelings of shame were closely linked to both social isolation and drinking. Under *A* (event), Jim identified a recent event that sparked his awareness of his shameful feelings—he remembered that his last visit with his wife was an occasion of intense shame. Jim reflected on his thoughts in response to his wife's visit, and wrote them out under *B* (thoughts):

- I should be able to fix my wife's feelings.
- It's awful to see her cry.
- I should have known better than to become an alcoholic.
- What a miserable person I am.

Understanding the basic tools of RET, Jim disputed his logic by writing a critique of his thinking under *D* (dispute).

- Who says I should be able to fix my wife's feelings? I can't control her emotions.
- It's unpleasant to see her cry, and I wish she didn't have to go through this. Perhaps her tears will bring her some emotional relief.
- Alcoholism is rooted in my biological makeup. It's not a matter of willpower. Stop "shoulding" on yourself!
- I'm a fallible, worthwhile human. I have been strug-

gling with this miserable disease. I'm not a miserable person.

As Jim questioned his own thinking, he formulated a goal to help guide his behavior *(E)*. Jim recognized his need to provide emotional support to his wife while reducing his shame. Consequently, he listed the following constructive actions he could take to reach his goal:

• Express my concern and support directly to my wife.
• Invite her to participate in a couples' communications workshop at the local mental health center.
• Support my wife's involvement in a support group that addresses her needs.
• Complete two additional RET work sheets to identify specific ways I continue to shame myself.

Jim soon learned that by consciously challenging his beliefs and changing his behaviors, he was able to reduce his feelings of shame while providing emotional support to his wife. As Jim accepted his powerlessness over alcohol, he also recognized his other limitations. He was indeed fallible, but certainly not "bad" or "awful." Jim came to believe that it was human to make mistakes, to have limited control over one's life, and to have an illness like alcoholism. By accepting his humanity, Jim took an important first step in building a foundation for recovery while alleviating his self-reproach, unrealistic demands, and feelings of shame.

Putting It All Together

Here are six important things to remember about shame:

1. Shame is a pervasive feeling of worthlessness. Shame is different from guilt; it is not a simple reaction to our misbehavior. Shame is often a chronic feeling of inadequacy, emptiness, and self-doubt.

2. Shame is often rooted in childhood and adolescence, stemming from an unhealthy family system. The child or adolescent believes that severe family criticism is justified and grows up believing he or she is without worth or value. We were powerless over what we learned as a child.

3. Shame can also be a consequence of addiction. The inability to stop or control an addictive behavior frequently leads us to devalue our worth.

4. Intense feelings of shame result in self-defeating behaviors, such as social withdrawal or isolation, and addictive behavior, such as binge eating, compulsive gambling, or excessive drinking. Therefore, shame is a risk factor for relapse.

5. Shame usually involves a "judge within" who demands rigid performance and shames us when these demands go unmet. Shame often involves a swing from perfectionistic expectations to self-condemnation. The "judge within" actually represents our own belief systems.

6. Since shame is invented and learned, it can be un-invented and unlearned. By using resources available to us including basic RET tools, we can

successfully reduce our feelings of shame—that is, experience shame less intensely and less often.

A RET Assignment

Now it's your turn! As with any new behavior, you need to practice reducing your feelings of shame. Your task is to complete an RET assignment. You may want to use a notebook. Here are a few tips to consider as you write out an assignment.

Identify shame. First, start by identifying the upsetting feeling of shame. Consider the self-defeating behaviors commonly related to shame. Be specific. Think of an example from your own experience.

Identify the event. Next, identify the activating event. Think of a time when a particular action encouraged you to feel shame more intensely. It might have been feedback during group therapy, or a comment that your spouse made. In any event, be as objective, concrete, and specific as possible in identifying the event (*A*).

Identify your thoughts and feelings. Your next task is to identify your thoughts (*B*). Review the examples of Ellen and Jim. Usually, feelings of shame (*C*) are triggered by unrealistic demands, a tendency to "awfulize," and self-devaluation.

Critique your thinking. Dispute your logic (*D*). Here, critique your thoughts, question your logic, and develop a more rational alternative.

State your goals. Consider your goals for the situation. Of course, you prefer to feel shame less often and less intensely. It's better to allow yourself to feel sorry and regretful instead of shamed and self-doubting. Reducing shame is certainly an important goal for a contented recovery. Oftentimes, this goal helps to guide us in acting constructively.

Taking action. List all the constructive actions you could take in order to reach your goal (*E*). Be as specific and concrete as possible. Number the list and keep it simple, but focus on action.

Now that you have completed a written RET assignment, your next task is to share this assignment with others. Look for additional feedback regarding your thinking *(B)*. Ask your peers if there is something you've missed. Might they have additional ideas for disputing your logic *(D)*? Perhaps one of your peers has an additional action to list under *E*. Use the RET assignment as a catalyst in discussing your feelings, shame-based attitudes, and emerging alternative belief systems. The more you involve others in the process, the more quickly you are likely to learn ways to reduce feelings of shame.

Don't forget to consider other self-help methods in attacking your feelings of shame. Remember, Ellen used self-affirmations to reinforce her emerging attitude of self-respect. Jim, for instance, identified ways that he "took control" and blocked acceptance of both his alcoholism and his humanity. Both Jim and Ellen took care to inform their sponsors that shame was a relapse risk.

Don't give up easily. You've probably had many years of practicing shame-based behaviors. It will take a lot of practice to find new self-affirming behaviors. A number of resources can be helpful, such as self-help support groups, individual and group therapy, long-term counseling, and relapse-prevention groups. By modifying attitudes and changing behavior, you can reduce your feelings of shame, lessen your risk for relapse, and open yourself to the joys of a healthier, happier life.

Suggested Reading

Ellis, Albert, and R. A. Harper. *A New Guide to Rational Living.* Hollywood, Calif.: Wilshire Books, 1975.

Ellis, Albert. *How to Stubbornly Refuse To Make Yourself Miserable About Anything—Yes, Anything!* Secaucus, N.J.: Lyle Stuart, 1988.

Hafner, A. Jack. *It's Not as Bad as You Think: Coping with Upset Feelings.* Center City, Minn.: Hazelden Educational Materials, 1981.

Kranzler, G. D. *You Can Change How You Feel.* New York: Institute for Rational-Emotive Therapy, 1975.

Maultsby, Maxie C., Jr. *Help Yourself to Happiness.* New York: Institute for Rational Living, 1975.

Thornton, Kellen. *Learning to Live with Emotions.* Center City, Minn.: Hazelden Educational Materials, 1987.

Young, Howard. *A Rational Counseling Primer.* New York (45 East 65th Street, New York, N.Y. 10021): Institute for Rational-Emotive Therapy, 1974.

THE TWELVE STEPS
OF ALCOHOLICS ANONYMOUS*

1. We admitted we were powerless over alcohol—that our lives had become unmanageable.
2. Came to believe that a Power greater than ourselves could restore us to sanity.
3. Made a decision to turn our will and our lives over to the care of God *as we understood Him.*
4. Made a searching and fearless moral inventory of ourselves.
5. Admitted to God, to ourselves, and to another human being the exact nature of our wrongs.
6. Were entirely ready to have God remove all these defects of character.

* The Twelve Steps of A.A. are taken from *Alcoholics Anonymous,* 3rd ed., published by A.A. World Services, Inc., New York, N.Y., 59-60. The Twelve Steps are reprinted and adapted with permission of Alcoholics Anonymous World Services, Inc. Permission to reprint and adapt the Twelve Steps does not mean that Alcoholics Anonymous has reviewed or approved the contents of this publication, nor that AA agrees with the views expressed herein. The views expressed herein are solely those of the authors. AA is a program of recovery from alcoholism. Use of the Twelve Steps in connection with programs and activities that are patterned after AA, but that address other problems, does not imply otherwise.

7. Humbly asked Him to remove our shortcomings.

8. Made a list of all persons we had harmed, and became willing to make amends to them all.

9. Made direct amends to such people wherever possible, except when to do so would injure them or others.

10. Continued to take personal inventory and when we were wrong promptly admitted it.

11. Sought through prayer and meditation to improve our conscious contact with God *as we understood Him,* praying only for knowledge of His will for us and the power to carry that out.

12. Having had a spiritual awakening as the result of these steps, we tried to carry this message to alcoholics, and to practice these principles in all our affairs.

✳
"EASY DOES IT, BUT DO IT"
with Hazelden Books

THE 12 STEPS TO HAPPINESS by Joe Klaas

                      36787 $4.95

BARRIERS TO INTIMACY: For People Torn by Addiction and Compulsive Behavior by Gayle Rosellini and Mark Worden

                      36735 $4.99

BACK FROM BETRAYAL: Recovering From His Affairs by Jennifer Schneider, M.D.   36786 $4.95

LIVING RECOVERY: Inspirational Moments for 12 Step Living by Men and Women in Anonymous Fellowships

                      36785 $4.99

COMPULSIVE EATERS AND RELATIONSHIPS by Aphrodite Matsakis   36831 $4.99

CREATING CHOICES: How Adult Children Can Turn Today's Dreams Into Tomorrow's Reality by Sheila Bayle-Lissick and Elise Marquam Jahns   37378 $4.99

SHOWING UP FOR LIFE: A Recovering Overeater's Triumph Over Compulsion by Heidi Waldrop

                      37379 $4.99

AGAINST THE WALL: Men's Reality in a Codependent Culture by John Hough and Marshall Hardy

                      37454 $4.99

TALK, TRUST, AND FEEL: Keeping Codependency Out of Your Life by Melody Beattie et al.   37455 $4.99

MEN'S WORK: How to Stop the Violence That Tears Our Lives Apart by Paul Kivel   37939 $5.99

JOURNEYNOTES: Writing For Recovery and Spiritual Growth by Richard Solly and Roseann Lloyd

                      37852 $4.99

FROM ANGER TO FORGIVENESS *by Earnie Larsen with Carol Larsen Hegarty*   37982 $4.99

"I WON'T WAIT UP TONIGHT": What to Do to Take Care of Yourself When You're Living With an Alcoholic or an Addict *by Terence Williams*   37940 $4.99

GRATITUDE: Reaffirming the Good Things in Life (Hardcover Gift Book and 52 Gratitude Cards) *by Melody Beattie*   38126 $16.00

CHANGE IS A CHOICE (Hardcover Gift Book and 52 Change Cards) *by Earnie Larsen with Carol Larsen Hegarty*   38128 $16.00

LIVING WELL: A Twelve Step Response to Chronic Illness and Disability *by Martha Cleveland*   38519 $4.99

I DESERVE RESPECT: Confronting and Challenging Shame *Lewis Anderson, ed.*   38518 $5.50

Coming in November 1993
DESIGN FOR GROWTH: Twelve Steps for Adult Children *by Veronica Ray*   38517 $4.99

These bestsellers are available in your local bookstore, or order by calling, toll-free, 1-800-733-3000 to use your major credit card.

Price and order numbers subject to change without notice. Valid in U.S. only.

✳

For information about the Hazelden Foundation and its treatment and professional services call 1-800-328-9000. 24 Hour Fax line 1-612-257-1331. Outside U.S. call (612) 257-4010.